The Coming
that Completes
the Story

Cover to Cover Bible Discovery

1 & 2 THESSALONIANS

The Coming
that Completes
the Story

PHILIP GREENSLADE

Published 2004 by CWR, Waverley Abbey House, Waverley Lane, Farnham, Surrey GU9 8EP.

See back of book for list of National Distributors.

Unless otherwise indicated, all Scripture references are from the Holy Bible: New International Version (NIV), copyright © 1973, 1978, 1984 by the International Bible Society.

Other Scripture quotations are marked:
NRSV: New Revised Standard Version, copyright © 1989
The Message, copyright © 1993, 1994, 1995, 1996, 2000, 2001, 2002
Phillips: J.B. Phillips The New Testament in Modern English, © 1960, 1972, J.B. Phillips, Fount Paperbacks

Concept development, editing, design and production by CWR.

Cover image: Alamy

Printed in Finland by W.S. Bookwell.

ISBN 1-85345-305-6

Contents

Preface

Paul's *first letter to the Thessalonians* was very likely the earliest of his letters to the churches. In this vivid and intimate letter, Paul shares his heart with the believers in the 'model' church he has founded. Reverberating through the letter is the hope and challenge offered to us by the return of Jesus, his *parousia* – as Paul terms it.

In his *second letter*, too, the Day of the Lord is an awesome prospect which, Paul insists, must shape the way that Christians think, feel and behave, so that God's future determines every aspect of our present way of life.

How strange all this seems in the current climate of evangelical and charismatic Christianity in the West. Modern evangelicals rightly reacted to the pious other-worldliness of an earlier generation, which perhaps had its head in the clouds. Let's 'walk the talk', we said; let's not to be so heavenly minded as to be of no earthly use. Fresh moves were made to apply the gospel to the 'here and now' of daily living, and 'how-to' books became the staple diet.

But as A.J. Conyers says in his aptly titled book *The Eclipse of Heaven*, such a move can easily degenerate into what is barely distinguishable from secularism. 'In a secular society,' Conyers observes, 'the centrifugal force continually presses away from the center out to the periphery, from the essential question of purpose to the peripheral question of the means and the technique.'[1]

So the Thessalonian letters force us to lift our eyes to the far horizon of ultimate issues, reminding us that it is God's future that determines our present.

For sure, P.T. Forsyth was eerily prophetic when he said: 'If *within* us we find nothing *over* us we succumb to what is *around* us.'[2]

The printed extracts from the Bible are from the NIV in the main. Departures from that are my own translation, unless otherwise marked.

My thanks are due once more to the able team of editors and designers at CWR for their craftsmanship, and of course, to Mary for her indefatigable support of an often flagging husband and writer.

As we re-explore the treasures in the Thessalonian correspondence, I pray that your hope may be renewed and your energies replenished as, together, we discover more of the living Lord and his life-giving truth.

Philip Greenslade
2004

Six things worth knowing about Paul's letters to the Thessalonians

The Thessalonian letters were written to Christians living in the most important city in Macedonia

Situated at the convergence of several important trade routes including the *Via Egnatia*, Thessalonica was capital of the whole province. Thessalonica had been rewarded for supporting Octavian in the Civil War by being granted the status of a 'free city', not ruled directly by Rome or occupied by a permanent Roman garrison but able to strike its own coinage and with its own appointed rulers whom Luke, with historical accuracy, calls the 'politarchs' (Acts 17:8). Thessalonica was for this reason intensely loyal to Rome and all the more sensitive to any seemingly anti-Roman sentiment.

Evidence exists for emperor worship in the city, alongside the major Egyptian cults of Serapis and Isis, those of the Greek gods such as Dionysus, and the cult of Cabirus. This was the city in 49–50 AD – about to hear the good news of Jesus for the first time!

The Thessalonian letters were written to Christians living in a vibrant and cosmopolitan community

As the administrative centre of the region and with the finest natural harbour in the Aegean, Thessalonica attracted trade and immigrants from all over the ancient world, swelling its population at the time to an estimated 60,000.

We know that women occupied a significant position in Macedonian society and the conversion of any of these noble women would have caused alarm among the elite (Acts 17:4). Cultural tensions made for a stimulating if unstable mix of foreign gods and religions, including Judaism.

The thriving seaport spawned a host of trade-guilds, each the centre of a lively and jealously guarded social life, with mutual support societies and regular feasts and banquets held in honour of the appropriate deity. Here Paul arrived to set up his workshop in the marketplace.

The first of the Thessalonian letters was written because Paul's stay in the city had been so short

Beyond the three Sabbaths when he had originally preached the gospel in the synagogue, Paul had spent perhaps as little as *four to six months* establishing the church in Thessalonica. He had stayed long enough for his apostolic lifestyle to be observed and copied (1 Thess. 2:9), and for him to receive gifts from the Philippians on at least two occasions (Phil. 4:16).

But it was all too brief, and his hasty departure had perhaps raised the suspicion that he was a 'fly-by-night' preacher, here today and gone tomorrow, only too quick to leave town at the slightest hint of trouble. Since then, time enough had elapsed for the fame of the Thessalonian Christians to have reached Achaia and Corinth from where Paul was writing (1 Thess. 1:7).

But Paul had nevertheless become very anxious as to how the Thessalonians were doing, and sent Timothy to find out. Timothy's name does not appear to have been included in the 'banning order' for which Jason stood bond (Acts 17:9) and he was therefore able to revisit the city, though Paul was not. Timothy returns with good news (1 Thess. 3:6) and Paul is prompted to thanksgiving and an intense desire to visit the Thessalonian Christians again (1 Thess. 3:9–10).

Unable to visit, he writes the first letter, which, when read aloud, will effectively stand in for his presence. So he writes perhaps only six or eight months after he had left to reassure the Thessalonians about his integrity and his deep affection for them.[3]

The Thessalonian letters were written to strengthen the Christians in time of affliction

Paul reminds the Thessalonians of his warning when he was with them that *suffering* 'comes with the territory'. It followed Paul himself around, faced Paul and his converts from the start in Thessalonica and had a long history (1 Thess. 2:1–2, 14–16; 3:3–4; 2 Thess. 1:4–5).

What was the nature of this 'affliction' which the Thessalonians were undergoing? Perhaps it was not at this stage systematic, physical ill-treatment. Rather it was almost certainly the social shame and dishonour heaped on people who had broken the conventions of idolatry and infringed the exclusive claims of Roman imperial power (1 Thess. 1:9–10). In Michael Holmes' words:

'Suffering' indicates the socio-religious dislocation, conflict, persecution, and/or ostracization experienced by the new converts as a result of turning to a new and socially suspect religion. The refusal of new Christian converts to participate in 'normal' social and cultic activities and the exclusivity of their claim to worship the only 'living and true God' ([1 Thess.] 1:9) would have left non-Christian friends feeling offended, resentful or betrayed; similarly, family members would have viewed a refusal to maintain ancestral traditions as evidence of an appalling lack of concern for family responsibilities. Moreover, since civic peace, agricultural success, and freedom from natural catastrophe were thought to lie in the hands of the traditional gods, it was considered extremely dangerous to ignore or offend them.[4]

The Thessalonian letters were written to make good deficiencies in their faith, especially to do with the *parousia*

The *parousia* is clearly the theme that dominates the Thessalonian correspondence. It is usually translated 'coming' but in itself does not convey this idea. Rather *parousia* implies 'presence' or 'arrival'. Significantly, it was a word used in the Graeco-Roman world of the state visit of the emperor, governor or other leading dignitaries whose coming to town would arouse immense interest and would be attended with much pomp and ceremony.

When we speak – as Paul does – of the *parousia* of the Lord Jesus, we might translate it as the 'Great Arrival', although, to be sure, Jesus is 'coming', as it were, 'from the heavenly realm' to this earthly realm in a special way (1 Thess. 1:10; 4:16).

Now Paul had clearly taught the Thessalonians about this future fact as our blessed hope. The phrases 'you know' or 'as we have already told you' or 'you remember' remind the readers of what they already know (eg 1 Thess. 1:5; 2:1,2,5,9,11; 3:3–4; 4:2,6; 5:1–2). But Timothy has uncovered 'deficiencies in their faith' (see 1 Thess. 3:10), which must be made good. The missing link seems to have been in their hope for the future. In particular they are *worried about the fate of those who die in Christ before the* parousia *occurs.* Paul writes to fill out their hope with new teaching introduced by a phrase – 'we do not want you to be ignorant about ...' that he regularly uses for imparting fresh information (1 Thess. 4:13). No, Paul reassures them, those who are still alive when Christ returns will have no advantage over those who have died in Christ. What happens will happen to us *together!*

The second of the Thessalonian letters was sent to restate teaching about the Day of the Lord that had been misunderstood

Paul writes to encourage the Thessalonians in their continuing – perhaps intensifying – afflictions (2 Thess. 1:4). Above all he is passionately concerned to rectify what amounts to total distortion of his teaching on the Day of the Lord (2 Thess. 2:1–12). He writes in fiercely protective pastoral mood, bolstering the faith of the church by underlining how drastic is the division between the afflicted and those who are persecuting them when seen in the light of God's final judgment.

He picks up strongly on the issue of the 'unruly idle', which has evidently worsened since the first letter (2 Thess. 3:6–15; cf 1 Thess. 4:11–12).

Characteristically the whole letter is shot through with praise and prayer (2 Thess. 1:3ff.,11,12; 2:13,16–3:5,16).

The Thessalonian letters were written to the city where Paul had caused a riot!

This is how it had all begun ...

How it all began

[1]When they had passed through Amphipolis and Apollonia, they came to Thessalonica, where there was a Jewish synagogue. [2]As his custom was, Paul went into the synagogue, and on three Sabbath days he reasoned with them from the Scriptures, [3]explaining and proving that the Christ had to suffer and rise from the dead. 'This Jesus I am proclaiming to you is the Christ,' he said. [4]Some of the Jews were persuaded and joined Paul and Silas, as did a large number of God-fearing Greeks and not a few prominent women.

[5]But the Jews were jealous; so they rounded up some bad characters from the market-place, formed a mob and started a riot in the city. They rushed to Jason's house in search of Paul and Silas in order to bring them out to the crowd. [6]But when they did not find them, they dragged Jason and some other brothers before the city officials, shouting: 'These men who have caused trouble all over the world have now come here, [7]and Jason has welcomed them into his house. They are all defying Caesar's decrees, saying that there is another king, one called Jesus.' [8]When they heard this, the crowd and the city officials were thrown into turmoil. [9]Then they put Jason and the others on bail and let them go.

The Olympic Games had once been held in Thessalonica. The

harbour was a magnet for traders from all over the ancient world. The city swarmed with foreign faces and voices, merchants and ship owners. Their world was the bustling, competitive, settled world of trade and commerce, made possible by the sophisticated protection-racket that was Roman imperial peace and security.

Into this pulsating but well-established world in the fifth decade of the first century came three men whose visit would leave an indelible mark on Thessalonica.

Paul arrives in the city, accompanied by Silas and Timothy, after the 100-mile westward journey from Philippi where he had been persecuted (cf 1 Thess. 2:2). Luke tells us that as was his custom Paul preaches on three successive Sabbaths in the Jewish synagogue (Acts 17:1–9), seeking to persuade his hearers that Jesus is the Messiah.

Paul speaks in what would become familiar ways in his mission preaching. He reasons from the Scriptures, 'opening up' (a favourite term of Luke's; cf Luke 24:27,32) the story line of the Bible to show that it culminates in Jesus as the long-expected Jewish Messiah. Paul is no doubt by turns pugnacious and winsome as he lays out the evidence as one spreads a table with a feast.

When some Jews believe – Jason probably among them, together with a larger number of Greek God-fearers and a few prominent women – Jewish opposition flares up. A mob is recruited from among the idle unemployed to storm Jason's house – where the infant church may well be meeting – and, failing to find the apostolic team, drags Jason and some of the other believers before the city authorities. Apparently the apostles had already gained a reputation as troublemakers. News had almost certainly reached Thessalonica of the social unrest they had caused at Philippi.

Now they are accused of being those who 'have been turning the world upside down' (Acts 17:6, NRSV). From a cosy, Western Christian standpoint, talk of the Church 'turning the world upside down' may rise a wry smile. Granted the Church is called to comfort the disturbed and to disturb the comfortable, but the days are a distant memory when the gospel caused rioting on the streets! But for our brothers and sisters in Nigeria, Sudan or Indonesia or wherever the battle lines are sharply drawn, it may not come as a surprise.

In particular, the apostles are charged with what amounts to 'subversion' – infringing imperial decrees by speaking of Jesus as another king than Caesar. For this, Jason is fined and released on bail while the apostles slip out of town under cover of darkness.

Precisely what laws they infringed is not entirely clear from the text. But classical historian E.A. Judge connects the charge against the apostles with edicts issued by the Emperors Augustus and Tiberius against astrologers and diviners who might be tempted to forecast a change of emperor. In Rainer Reisner's words: 'Predictions concerning the health and life of the Emperor were particularly threatened with severe punishment not only in Rome but also in the provinces.'[5]

Paul's teaching on the *parousia* of the Lord Jesus Christ heralded a majestic and climactic event, which might well have been construed as an attempt to upstage the 'great arrivals' of Roman imperial representatives. Even though there is no record of the current emperor having made an ostentatious parade down the *Via Egnatia* to show off his glory to the provinces, there was an abundance of imperial images in sculpture and buildings to dazzle the populace of a city like Thessalonica with regal splendour.

But already in his public preaching and much more in his letters, Paul was hijacking standard imperial imagery and language and applying it to Jesus! Calling Jesus 'Lord and Saviour', awaiting his coming or *parousia* (the term used of the ceremonial arrival of an imperial delegate), proclaiming as official 'good news' the eternal salvation to be found in the presence and future of Jesus' 'kingdom' – all this posed a direct alternative to the vaunted 'peace and security' (1 Thess. 5:3, NRSV) guaranteed by the self-styled 'eternal city' of Rome. It was his experience in Thessalonica then that may well have honed Paul's language.

'Something dramatic happened in Thessalonica, something

which caused Paul to depict the Risen Jesus in distinctly *imperial imagery*.[6] As we have seen, this was the clash between two kingdoms which, when the gospel was announced, was enough to create social unrest.

Paul soon received sharp evidence of how even Jewish sensibilities had accommodated to the mind-set of the Roman Empire. And as for the pagans,

> he discovered just how tight Caesar's grip was on the hearts and minds of the humble tradespeople, craftspeople, slaves, servants, and day labourers, who had gradually drifted into the city from the rural areas over the previous few decades to find places for themselves in the highly stratified urban economy.[7]

But the gospel proved more than a match for an idolatrous world system. Proclaimed in the power of the Holy Spirit, the gospel of the Lordship of Jesus revolutionises the lives of idol worshippers, turning them into followers of the Risen Christ and servants of the living God (cf 1 Thess. 1:5–6,9–10; 2 Thess. 2:13–14). The word of the living God overrode any edict from the emperor (1 Thess. 2:13). The 'world' of these first Thessalonians converts was certainly turned upside down!

All of which gives modern Christians much pause for thought. This gripping narrative raises a crucial issue. *Why is the Church so often a reactionary rather than a revolutionary force?* Why is the Church so often found on the side of the state and uncritically serving its agenda? Why do we as Christians so readily acquiesce to the status quo in society?

'Turning the world upside down' clearly implies that the kingdom of God in which we serve invades our lives in order to put the world right-side up. So why, in Donald Kraybill's words, do we forget to ask why things are the way they are? 'The upside-down label encourages us to question the way things are.'[8]

Two broad answers may be suggested: the *nationalisation of the*

Church, and the *privatisation of faith*.

Nationalisation of the Church

In this process the Church uncritically associates itself with the prevailing culture. The Church becomes in effect the chaplain of society, blessing its values and baptising its structures.

In many cases, in the history of Western Christianity at least, the Church has got itself elected as the national religion. The interests of Church and State become intertwined and inseparable. The watershed for this happened barely three centuries after Paul planted a church in Thessalonica.

In 312 AD the Roman Empire, which Paul had been accused of defaming, wedded itself to Christianity as its official religion. What the Emperor Constantine did and the genuineness of his conversion have been much disputed since. Although only a minority report, there have always been those who have regarded this 'settlement' with only slight exaggeration as an unmitigated disaster.

Whatever the subtleties of the debate, there is no doubt that the picture of Constantinian Christianity as an all-embracing institution is a far cry from that of the dynamic movement which made such waves in first-century Macedonia.

The recent history of Bosnia or Northern Ireland offers tragic examples of the way in which Christianity – or some version of it – has been commandeered to give respectability and indeed divine sanction to all kinds of ruthless nationalistic movements.

Privatisation of faith

The other reason why the Church is not seen as a revolutionary social force is that, in the Western world at least, Christianity has been effectively *privatised*.[9] With their roots in the Pietistic movements of the eighteenth century, evangelical Christians have always been vulnerable to this tendency. These movements were genuine renewals of the Church by the Spirit, which arose as a protest against a dead, formal church and restored emphasis on the new birth, individual faith and personal experience of salvation.

There is so much for which to give thanks in this history that it seems churlish to criticise. But such renewal always carried with it the danger that its view of Christian experience might become so focused on personal transformation that salvation would come to be seen as a means of escape from the world.

Mix this with lurid scenarios of the imminent end of the world, and you have a recipe for self-imposed irrelevance. After all when Armageddon is round the corner why bother laying claims on society or – as it is often stated – why waste time rearranging the deck chairs on the *Titanic*? Forget the ship; get as many souls into the lifeboat of the Church as possible.

Of course, the ship of state doesn't sink and the next generation of Christians is left to bemoan the fact that the secular humanists have occupied all the seats of power in government and business and are the chief opinion-formers in education and the media. The steady march of secularisation of Western societies has accelerated this marginalising of Christianity to the fringes of society, where it is tolerated as a private leisure pursuit.

Os Guinness defines 'privatisation' as

> the process by which modernisation produces a cleavage between the public and private spheres of life and focuses the private sphere as the special area reserved for the expression of individual freedom and fulfilment.[10]

This is tolerance of a sort but it conceals a real danger for the gospel. As Os Guinness warns, if we go along with such a tolerance, then we have sold out. 'Far from being an area of true choice and creativity', he writes,

> the modern private sphere is all too often a sort of harmless play area, a sort of spiritual 'Indian reservation' … a homeland for separated spiritual development set up obligingly by the

architects of secular society's apartheid.[11]

As Paul makes clear in his letters, embracing the gospel is not about making a lifestyle choice but breaking with idols and social conventions in a way that settles one's eternal destiny!

No one reading this today outside the West in, say, Nigeria or Singapore may feel the warnings apply to them. But the danger remains. Within our tolerated 'corral', wild churches are tamed and the gospel domesticated.

The only answer to this is a fresh baptism of the Spirit into the reality that there *is* 'another king than Caesar'. To him every Caesar and every citizen is answerable.

When the Confessing Church in the Germany of the 1930s resisted Nazi pressure to toe the state's line, it did so in the boldly declared conviction that rejected 'the false notion that there could be areas of our life in which we would not belong to Jesus Christ but to other lords'. The issues at stake are seldom so clear-cut as that but the challenge remains. As John Yoder consistently maintained, 'A church that is not "against the world" in fundamental ways has nothing worth saying to and for the world.'[12]

Donald Kraybill places the challenge squarely before us:

> The corporate life of the people of God will be visible and external … Freed from the grip of right-side up kingdoms, we salute a new King and sing a new song. We pledge allegiance to a new and already-present kingdom. We are citizens of a future that is already breaking in. We are the ones who turn the world up-side down because we know there is another King named Jesus.[13]

Whether in safety or in danger, to be worthy of that kingdom and that king is our true Christian calling (2 Thess. 1:5,11). And as we await our King's arrival to enact heaven's will on earth, 'your kingdom come' is our prayer and our sure and certain hope.

Outline of the letters to the Thessalonians

1 Thessalonians

1:1–10	Converted to His coming
2:1–3:10	Crowned by His coming
3:11–4:12	Challenged by His coming
4:13–18	Comforted by His coming
5:1–11	Confounded by His coming
5:12–28	Completed at His coming

2 Thessalonians

1:1–5	Great news about the Church
1:6–10	Good news of God's justice

1 THESSALONIANS

1:1–10 Converted to His coming

1:1

¹Paul, Silas and Timothy,

To the church of the Thessalonians in God the Father and the Lord Jesus Christ:

Grace and peace to you.

'Nothing has changed but everything is different.' So it feels when God invades our lives with His transforming power and love. So it was for Paul and his friends even when it came to letter-writing. They begin by naming themselves and sending greetings in the time-honoured way.

But if the style is familiar there is nothing conventional about the content. Here is no formal greetings-card sentimentality but breathtaking theological conviction. This simple letter-heading opens to us another world.

These three – Paul and Silas (or to use his Latin name, Silvanus), together with their younger companion Timothy – are pioneer preachers and apostles of the greatest news the world has ever heard! Paul is the famous one and yet the fact that the letter is written in the second person plural as 'we' and 'us' speaks volumes for the way the gospel of God's love in Jesus has changed human relationships.

In this family, hierarchy counts for little. Paul is the undoubted leader but he shares the credits with his faithful friend, Silas, and his much-travelled delegate, Timothy, and only twice does he single himself out (1 Thess. 2:18; 5:27). The letter must be read out aloud to the gathered congregation in Thessalonica because it was substituting for Paul's own presence and apostolic authority.

'To the church of the Thessalonians in God the Father and the

Lord Jesus Christ …' What a story that tells! Bible exposition in the synagogue in Thessalonica, gospel preaching in the marketplace, witnessing for Jesus in the workshop – and meeting and worshipping and eating together in Jason's house – and it all ended in riots and banning orders and a hurried exit to Berea. But the Church had been planted there and was flourishing!

So Paul writes to the *ekklesia* made up of Thessalonian believers. Paul's choice of the word '*ekklesia*' is deliberate; there were alternatives which would have likened the Christian community to a trade-guild or social body. To understand something of what Paul has in mind in using this terminology, we might usefully distinguish the *roots* of the concept and the *context* in which Paul is using it.

- The *roots* of the concept of *ekklesia* are undoubtedly in the Old Testament Scriptures where Israel is viewed as the 'called-out' people of God, 'the assembly of the Lord' (Hebrew *quhal*, cf Acts 7:38). The Thessalonian believers in Messiah Jesus can know they are loved by the One Creator God and form part of His chosen people (1 Thess. 1:4).
- The *context* in which Paul is using the word '*ekklesia*' is the highly charged political atmosphere of the Graeco-Roman world. There, the word was used of the citizen-assemblies that governed the city-states in Mediterranean society.

Paul's choice of language then is highly specific, political and provocative.

Think of church as political assemblies, communities of the Empire of God, announcing the good news of the Lord Jesus as King, offering worship not to the present emperor but to the Last Emperor Jesus, welcoming and serving one another in sacrificial love as a sign and foretaste of that great final Empire of God to which shall come those of every tongue from every nation and tribe who have answered the call of grace.

As Stanley Hauerwas and William Willimon put it, 'Think of Easter as a political rally. Think of Sunday worship, our handling of the broken bread and the shed blood, as our attempt to get our politics right.'[14]

In Michael Gorman's words,

> These communities Paul founded, the *ekklesiai* (plural), are, individually, alternative assemblies to the local *polis*, and, corporately an international network of communities constituting an alternative empire to that of Rome.[15]

No wonder there were riots in Thessalonica! No wonder the apostles often found themselves in hot water and cold cells. Not surprising, is it, that they were accused of 'subverting the empire', of 'turning the world upside down' or of 'proclaiming another Lord than Caesar'? Not really surprising then that early Christians such as the Thessalonians accepted social hostility and suffering as the cost of discipleship.

The secret was their double life: they had their homes and businesses in Thessalonica but they lived '*in God the Father and the Lord Jesus Christ*'. They existed in another realm of reality altogether.

And notice how one preposition, 'in', covers God the Father and the Lord Jesus Christ. This is the very highest Christology possible; Jesus, crucified not more than 20 years before as a rebel against Rome and a false Messiah, is now bracketed without embarrassment with the One Creator God. And that not at the end of a long process of development but right from the start, in the earliest letter Paul writes!

1:2-3

[2]We always thank God for all of you, mentioning you in our prayers. [3]We continually remember before our God and Father

your work produced by faith, your labour prompted by love, and your endurance inspired by hope in our Lord Jesus Christ.

Paul gives thanks for the new Thessalonian church in God and Jesus. Then in what will become a trademark of his letters – a prayer report – he says that he continually remembers them when he prays.

How could he forget them? For these are *memorable Christians* notable for a triad of virtues and actions.

1. *Faith's work* – the good works we do are the only lasting evidence of faith we have. Paul and James are at one on this (James 2:18–20). And it takes faith to continue to do good works; faith in future grace to sustain us in what we begin to do; faith in the final rewards that await us at the end of the race; faith to believe that a cup of cold water given now in His name matters in the great scheme of things.

2. *Love's labour* – Paul can speak like this of the work of love because love is not a misty-eyed feeling but a self-giving action, demonstrated in the cross of Jesus and poured into us by the Holy Spirit. Such love becomes an energy that does things. This love works wonders. God's love truly changes everything.

3. *Hope's endurance* – 'hupomene' is the steadfastness and persistence which genuine hope instils in us. Love hopes all things, believes all things … and undergirding it all is a tough, hang-in-there endurance which is inspired by a hope fixed not on passing emotions or temporary moods of optimism but firmly on the Lord Jesus Christ. Hope is faith in future grace, which trusts that the work faith does will bear fruit. Hope is joyful resilience – the bounce-back factor, the come-up-smiling-and-determined factor. Hope breeds perseverance; it is the buoyancy that keeps faith and love afloat in turbulent times. True faith's work is never wasted, real love's labour is never lost, hope's resilience is never disappointed.

It is perhaps significant that the triad of virtues ends with hope since hope is the beating heart of the whole letter.

As so often in Paul's letters, the key themes are stated in the thanksgiving or prayer reports early in the letter. So here faith, love and hope are elaborated in 1 Thessalonians 2:8–3:12 (faith: 3:2,5,6,7,10; love: 2:8; 3:6,12; hope: 2:19) and again picked up in 4:9–5:22 (faith: 5:8; love: 4:9–10; 5:8,13; hope: 4:13ff.; 5:8; etc).

The phrase 'In the presence of our God and Father' (v.3a, NIV 'before …') is placed at the end of verse 3 in the Greek text. To what does it refer? Perhaps the Thessalonians' triad of good works? Or Paul's remembering and praying? Maybe both. Paul has just reminded them that everything they do in faithful, loving and hopeful service they do as the people who exist 'in God … and the Lord Jesus' (v.1) and he will later speak of the 'joy we have in the presence of our God because of you' (1 Thess. 3:9). Whether for apostle or people, God is our only audience.

In thinking of how well the Thessalonians are manifesting faith and love and hope, Paul recalls how it all began for the Thessalonians. That they have so quickly become credible and productive Christians is a testimony to their quality. In particular it highlights the effect of the gospel and how well the message was received.

1:4-6

[4]For we know, brothers loved by God, that he has chosen you, [5]because our gospel came to you not simply with words, but also with power, with the Holy Spirit and with deep conviction. You know how we lived among you for your sake. [6]You became imitators of us and of the Lord; in spite of severe suffering, you welcomed the message with the joy given by the Holy Spirit.

How the message came was crucial

The message came not with words only but 'with power, with the Holy Spirit', so that it carried 'deep conviction' (v.5). This is the effect of true gospel preaching. Whether the power of words in popular usage is under- or overestimated, I remain convinced that biblical preaching which testifies to the truth and is acted upon by the Holy Spirit is *powerfully* *'performative'*. In true preaching something is not merely *said*, something is *done!*

Preaching is a means of grace. It does not merely describe God's grace, but imparts it. Preaching is instructive by its very nature. It comes with clear and definable content to seize and convince the mind with full assurance of truth. But preaching is not primarily about imparting information. Preaching does not merely talk about God, it confronts us with God. It does not merely initiate a discussion about God but sets up an encounter with God. *Preaching is perfomative speech.* Notice too that part of its immediate power was the integrity and credibility of the preachers who were living samples of the truth of what they preached (v.5c).

How the message was received was vital

If how the message came was crucial, then how the message was received was vital too (v.6). The Thessalonians had received the gospel 'in spite of severe suffering' (v.6). In other words, they welcomed the good news of Jesus even though it cost them much to do so; it came with a price tag, social stigma attached, possible persecution to follow!

This tells us a lot about the kind of gospel they were offered. It was not the offer of a Christianised therapy to make them feel better about themselves; not the offer of a new spirituality which would neatly fit into their existing lifestyles to make them more comfortable or life more exciting. This was no placebo but the real thing, costing not less than everything both on God's part and on theirs!

This was true conversion – welcoming the message as the truth without regard to the consequences! And the consequences were inevitable – 'affliction' was the sign that followed the Word in New Testament times! Breaking with local religions and sitting light to Roman imperial claims and propaganda gave rise to suspicion and hostility.

'Knowing Jesus' was no private trip into mystical intimacy but aroused public resentment from relatives and former friends. If workmates or business clients gave you the cold shoulder or verbal abuse, it was because of the 'potentially anti-Roman, anti-establishment proclamation of Jesus the Messiah, crucified by the Romans, as the coming Ruler and Judge'.[16]

And the Thessalonians, in accepting the consequences of following Jesus, did so with an irrepressible *joy inspired by the Holy Spirit.*

1:7-10

> [7]And so you became a model to all the believers in Macedonia and Achaia. [8]The Lord's message rang out from you not only in Macedonia and Achaia – your faith in God has become known everywhere. Therefore we do not need to say anything about it, [9]for they themselves report what kind of reception you gave us. They tell how you turned to God from idols to serve the living and true God, [10]and to wait for his Son from heaven, whom he raised from the dead – Jesus, who rescues us from the coming wrath.

It was their extraordinary resilience despite affliction that made the Thessalonians a *model church*. They had been urged to consider the apostles and Jesus himself as examples to follow of faithfulness through suffering – 'You became imitators of us and of the Lord' (v.6a). Now in their turn, the Thessalonians became a model (*tupos*) to 'all the believers in Macedonia and Achaia' (v.7).

It is precisely their joyful embrace of the gospel amidst opposition and hostility that makes them an example of how to live the cruciform life. The Thessalonians are a model church not because they strut the 'catwalk' of prideful success, numerical or otherwise, but because they rejoice to confess the gospel in the bear-pit of spiritual warfare and social oppression. Notice how Paul describes their spreading fame: 'The Lord's message [the word of the Lord] rang out from you not only in Macedonia and Achaia – your faith in God has become known everywhere' (v.8).

The word translated 'rang out' or 'sounded forth' is a musical term sometimes applied to a trumpet sound. The music of His name resonates throughout the region because of the way the Thessalonians are faithfully living out the Christ-life together.

What made the Thessalonian church famous was not its expansion throughout the region. Not enough time had elapsed for that to be the reason. No: the fame which had spread was news of their radical conversion. The word of the Lord 'rang out' because of its dynamic impact on their lives. What grabbed the headlines in the Christian media everywhere was the total life-changing experience of the gospel in their lives. News of that spread like wildfire!

They had experienced a striking countercultural conversion (vv.9–10)

Every aspect of their conversion implies a radical break with convention and social norms:

- '... to God from idols to serve the living and true God ...'
  Turning from what is seen to be lifeless, unreal and false; turning not from one religion to another; but from 'nothing' to life-giving reality ... and with all the social consequences we have already mentioned of ostracism and hostility.
- '... to wait for [God's] Son ... Jesus ...' Turning from spending all in the present age, in a kingdom that can be shaken; and investing instead in a kingdom that cannot be shaken; taking the long view, and living for and in the light of the future glory

as we wait for Jesus to give out the prizes. His coming is guaranteed by His resurrection from the dead.

- '... *to be saved from ... coming wrath*' Turning from moral ignorance or rebellion to a realisation of eternal realities of a heavenly bliss to be gained and a hell to be avoided; converted from turning a blind eye to sin and its effects to a close-up view of sin and its consequences.

There's an old preacher's story that's worth repeating.

When faced with a rapidly advancing forest fire, and running away was not a safe option, the only remedy for the forest people was to set light to a circle of ground on which they stood. Then they would wait on the burnt-out patch of earth for the flames to surge up to the edge of their space, find nothing to consume and pass by. Later the fire even proved beneficial in renewing the earth.

Mark Buchanan applies the image well, 'Jesus Christ burned the earth with the cross. God poured out his wrath on his Son. If we take our stand there, the wrath to come will pass us by, and in its time will renew the very earth it devours. Don't even try to run. Just rest there, thankful'.[7]

'Turning the world upside down' was what the apostles were accused of in Thessalonica – and to induce pagans to turn 'from idols to serve the living and true God' is to do just that. Conversion is a complete 180-degree turnround. And as someone has said – a crucified man is facing only way! So Christians who have died with Christ have lives bent wholly in God's direction and, in particular, hearts turned towards the coming kingdom. They put their faith in future grace, which saves them from coming wrath into the arms of a coming Saviour.

We are converted to His coming or we are only half-converted, only half-turned. No one is truly converted until their focus is turned from their past – long forgiven by the cleansing blood – and from the present age, with all its idolatrous distractions, to wholehearted service of the true and living God and God's future.

How countercultural it all still is when radically experienced. Cutting loose from the social idolatries of consumerism, entertainment, materialism, sexual obsession and untrammelled self-expression. Relinquishing the gods we make in our own image that serve our interests, and surrendering ourselves to be the willing servants of the One true God.

And 'wait'! Who wants to wait? This is a countercultural stance if ever there was one, in a society that demands everything now, in instant satisfaction. Nor is this a temporal hope that means just waiting till tomorrow for things to get better. No: here is a waiting that stakes all on another world entirely; another realm – 'heaven' – and another time and place, no doubt long beyond our life span, when He shall come again who has once come to transfigure our world.

Here is a waiting in faith that disenchants us with all lesser satisfaction and glory, and prefers to fix its hopes on God's Son from heaven for final vindication and ultimate happiness. It is a trusting for a salvation not from bad feelings or bad memories or anything in this world alone but from the 'wrath of judgment' that awaits impenitent sinners. Who believes in that anymore? Who believes in being accountable to anything or anyone, let alone to a moral and holy God? The gospel of true grace that creates real conversion is as countercultural today as it ever was.

But this is the only gospel that converts. And this is the conversion that counts. From idolatrous, self-serving gods to God-centred and God-directed living. From quick-fix spiritualities to a life turned towards the future, with eyes that scan the horizon for the coming kingdom. From careless lives, unaccountable and promiscuous, to lives that realise with deepening grief not only the tragedy *in* the world but the tragedy *of* the world, doomed as it is to destruction.

Yes, to be converted is to cast oneself with hilarious relief on the mercy of God in Christ, who is the Saviour we need from the wrath to come and thankfully is the Saviour we have!

If the Thessalonians face shame, loss of honour and lowering social status in society, Paul reaffirms their value to God as His chosen, beloved and valued people (1 Thess. 1:4) and their growing reputation in the eyes of other believers for faithfulness and courage (v.7). In other words what costs them esteem among the pagans is precisely what gains them fame among their fellow-believers. Above all, their own eyes are fixed on the future, on the One who comes from heaven to save them from wrath and in doing so to vindicate them as God's own people.

To be converted to His coming is to see the world turned right-side up!

Prayer and Reflection

Our coming to You, Lord, is a coming full-circle –
   turning ...
   ... back to our true beginnings,
   ... back to where we belong,
   ... back to the source of our life.

Our coming to You is the great turning point –
   turning ...
   ... from shadowy illusion to substantial reality,
   ... from stagnant religion to streams of living water,
   ... from lies and spin to the fresh air of truth,
   ... from self-made idolatries to the true and living God.

Your coming again to us will complete the story.

Meanwhile, we wait,
   ... not for something to turn up but for a Son from heaven,
   ... not to get what we deserve but to receive the final grace.
We wait for the risenness of Jesus to spill over into the
resurrection of all our deadness.

Meanwhile, fill us afresh with Your Spirit so that we may resist
the temptation to settle for anything less than what the Son from
heaven wills to give us. Amen.

A.W. Tozer said that the essence of idolatry is thinking thoughts
of God that are unworthy of Him.

- What in your view are the idolatries that attract 'worship' in the
  modern world?
- How true is Jim Packer's statement that for Christians the only
  proof of past conversion is present convertedness?

2:1–3:10 Crowned by His coming

2:1–6

¹You know, brothers, that our visit to you was not a failure. ²We had previously suffered and been insulted in Philippi, as you know, but with the help of our God we dared to tell you his gospel in spite of strong opposition. ³For the appeal we make does not spring from error or impure motives, nor are we trying to trick you. ⁴On the contrary, we speak as men approved by God to be entrusted with the gospel. We are not trying to please men but God, who tests our hearts. ⁵You know we never used flattery, nor did we put on a mask to cover up greed – God is our witness. ⁶We were not looking for praise from men, not from you or anyone else.

How do we measure success? What constitutes honour and glory? These were important issues in the honour–shame culture that was first-century Thessalonica, a culture sensitive to every nuance of esteem or lack of it.

Paul feels the need to resort to a narrative defence of his actions and ministry both when he was with the Thessalonians and since leaving them. His visit was successful, he confidently asserts, for it left a viable and vibrant church there (v.1). But it was *the manner of his leaving* that was half the problem. In face of civic unrest and official complaints, Paul and Silas, we recall, had had to beat a hurried retreat from Thessalonica.

Now, there could be no question that the speedy exit from Thessalonica was simply a way to avoid suffering. If that kind of consideration had been in our hearts, Paul argues, we would never have come to you at all! 'We had previously suffered and been insulted in Philippi, as you know' (v.2). But that painful experience, he reminds them, did not deter the apostolic party. Paul is able to look the Thessalonians and any possible critics in the eye and say, 'We dared to tell you the gospel in spite of strong opposition.' This is a deeply moving cameo: even after such rough treatment at Philippi, Paul and Silas preached again, knowing the likely consequences.

But although his visit had not been 'in vain', the suspicion might still be levelled that the speed of his departure cast doubts on Paul's integrity. At the time, travelling preachers and itinerant orators had a very dubious reputation. Their appearance was more in the nature of entertainment than education. It was cynically assumed that their short and beguiling visits were usually followed by quick exits with bulging money pouches.

Dio Crysostom, a public speaker himself, some 25 years after Paul, criticised some wandering philosophers who, he said, 'merely utter a phrase or two, and then after railing at you rather than teaching you, they make a hurried exit, anxious lest before they had finished you may raise an out-cry and send them packing'.[18]

Part of Paul's 'conflict' (v.2) may have been the kind of opposition aroused by just such suspicions. In fact Dio Crysostom goes on to accuse the Cynics – the wandering philosophers – of exactly the things against which Paul defends himself here: error, impurity, deceit, flattery, courting honour and money-grabbing.[19]

Paul is not a rip-off merchant, out for a quick buck and leaving behind him a trail of social disorder (vv.3–6).

- His message was not error but truth from God;
- His motives were not impure;
- His methods were not manipulative.

At this point Paul employs a series of vivid *pictures to describe his ministry.*

He regards himself as a *steward*, 'entrusted with the gospel' (v.4). Paul never sees himself or his fellow-apostles as self-made but as *God-made* men. Paul speaks for Silas and Timothy as well as himself. God's messenger is bold and audacious, defying convention, because God has sent him. He wants to win people to his cause but he will not curry favour with them out of his own emotional need for their applause. His security comes from being 'approved by God' (v.4). Like a metal expert testing the quality of the material he is working with so God 'tests the hearts' (*dokimazo* twice) of his servants and approves them as trustworthy stewards of his affairs.

Here Paul gives us an awe-inspiring glimpse of the *God-examined, God-centred, God-directed life*. Here is pictured a human life lived wide open to God's scrutiny; lived out, not in fearful shadows, but transparently in the full light of God's gaze. It sounds intimidating but, as Paul describes it, begins to feel immensely liberating. Having his entire existence shaped and defined by God does not make Paul craven or inhibited. On the contrary, it is precisely what frees him to be bold and to take risks.

Knowing God's approval, he need not set out to flatter anyone (v.5).

Secure in God's provision, he never lets greed motivate him (v.5).

Resisting the pressure to conform to the values of an honour–shame society, Paul does not seek his own glory. He can readily forego an easy popularity in order to bring pleasure to God (v.6).

No one knew this better than his Thessalonian converts (v.5), and above all, 'God is our witness' (v.5). The apostles were not the shifty salesmen of religious products, but the approved and appointed spokesmen for God. Their message was not skilfully concocted to meet the felt needs of their hearers or tickle the fancy of those hooked on the latest fad in trendy spirituality.

Thessalonica had plenty of that to offer. The city was awash with exotic cults and niche-marketed religions. But what the Thessalonians had never heard before and needed most of all to hear was an authentic word from the true and living God. It was this the apostles offered and to this the converts in Thessalonica eagerly turned. What they heard and what changed them was – as Paul mentions three times – 'the gospel of God' (vv.2,8,9).

The charlatans made a fleeting impression and were gone; the apostles approved by this God were 'heralds' of good news from the One Creator God which, when received, made lasting and eternal impact. In all this, although they preached to crowds, the apostles lived as if God were their only audience.

2:7-12

As apostles of Christ we could have been a burden to you, [7]but we were gentle among you, like a mother caring for her little children. [8]We loved you so much that we were delighted to share with you not only the gospel of God but our lives as well, because you had become so dear to us. [9]Surely you remember, brothers, our toil and hardship; we worked night and day in order not to be a burden to anyone while we preached the gospel of God to you.
[10]You are witnesses, and so is God, of how holy, righteous and blameless we were among you who believed. [11]For you know that we dealt with each of you as a father deals with his own children, [12]encouraging, comforting and urging you to live lives worthy of God, who calls you into his kingdom and glory.

In the next image, somewhat surprisingly, Paul pictures the apostles as *children or babes* (v.7). There is at this point a technical matter of translation to be decided, involving a difference of one letter, and depending on which manuscript you follow. The word Paul used may have been either *epioi*, which means 'gentle'; or *nēpioi*, which means 'infants' or 'babes'. The NIV and others opt for the less well-attested reading because they feel it fits the context, and so translate 'gentle'. Gordon Fee, whose massive expertise includes textual criticism, argues strongly for following the best-supported reading in the manuscripts, and opts for *nēpioi*, 'infants' or 'babes'.[20] So the text might read: '... we became children among you ...'
What might this mean as applied to the apostolic witness? It

means that God-given boldness should never be confused with brashness or sheer bravado. Spiritual machismo is not essential to true apostolic work. Nor is there any need to be devious.

Speaking the truth, Paul and Silas could afford to be straightforward, innocent and childlike. They were free from the need to be overbearing or burdensome. Although they could 'have thrown their weight around' – as the Greek graphically suggests – they did not. Instead they came to the Thessalonians with almost childlike simplicity and disingenuousness.

Almost immediately the picture changes to that of a *nursing mother* (vv.7b–9). Paul uses this metaphor to express deep affection for the Thessalonian church and to characterise his apostolic ministry to it. It is like a mother's care and self-giving love, which is truly a sacrificing of her own life for her child (v.8). It means hard work and hardship, sleepless nights, a genuine laying down of one's life in daily instalments (v.9). Many of us cannot forget what our mothers did.

I grew up in the immediate post-war years in Britain when food and money were scarce. My mother gave me food off her own plate to make sure I lacked nothing. She also worked with her hands. I can still picture her in freezing weather, with raw and reddened hands, squeezing hand-washed clothes through a hand-operated mangle, which stood under a lean-to outside our back door, exposed to the worst of the winter climate. And I know she never regretted it or complained. She did it for love.

What Paul is picturing is authentic, incarnational ministry. Evangelism in this mode is not the beaming by satellite of slick shows into the sealed-off living-rooms of the terminally bored. Instead it is real, hands-on ministry, eating and working alongside the people you are seeking to reach. The old missionaries, now much derided, never trusted to long-distance calls. For them as for Paul, the gospel was an embodied message, the good news of the outpoured life of the very Son of God, endorsed by the outpoured lives of his witnesses. Such ministry is costly and drains energy; but it is a real impartation of life to others (cf 2 Cor. 4:12).

Interestingly, Paul admits that he had not wanted to be a financial burden to the Thessalonians as he preached the gospel to them (1 Thess. 2:9). In this he was flexible. He accepted monetary support from the Philippians (Phil. 4:14–19) and relished the experience of *koinonia* (fellowship) it gave him. But he refused to be beholden to the Corinthians (eg 2 Cor. 11:7–9), who wanted to put him under obligation by their financial support and were insulted when he turned them down!

Paul's was a tough-and-tender grace but the nourishment and nurture of his children in the faith forged a deep and lasting bond of love between with them. That for him was reward enough.

Paul next turns to the image of a *father* (v.11). This is not to be feared as an authoritarian, hierarchical or repressive picture. Fatherhood could certainly carry these connotations in the ancient world. But at best fathers were sources of wisdom and served to educate their offspring in the ways and practices of social and civic life.

Paul captures well the atmosphere of a healthy parent–child relationship when he speaks of 'encouraging, comforting and urging you to live lives worthy of God' (v.12a), 'showing you step by step how to live well before God' (*The Message*). Paul had 'dealt' with each of them 'as a father deals with his own children', 'stimulating your faith and courage and giving you instruction' (Phillips).

This fatherly role explains why, in common with ancient practice, Paul can quite naturally and with no trace of egoism, speak of the Thessalonians 'imitating him' (1 Thess. 1:6). That's what children were meant to do. Paul and his team had an integrity worth emulating, which made them a credible source of 'fatherly' influence (1 Thess. 2:10).

Rodney Clapp helpfully advises us to take heart in our postmodern world as the printed word loses some of its dominance. He points out that 'how-to' manuals exist only in print cultures and reminds us that 'in oral cultures, trades are learned through apprenticeship, through observation and practice with minimal verbalised instruction'. He goes on to urge that:

> Christian discipleship is better served by the model of apprenticeship than the model of the how-to manual. Christians best mature in the living of faith when they are apprenticed to wise Christians they can observe, question and work with in a range of concrete situations.

Books on how to apply the Bible to life issues, Clapp suggests, are a poor substitute for Christian formation forged in a faithful community through apprenticed discipleship.[21] Current interest in modelling leadership and in spiritual mentoring are hopeful signs perhaps that the Church is moving in the right direction.[22]

2:13-16

[13]And we also thank God continually because, when you received the word of God, which you heard from us, you accepted it not as the word of men, but as it actually is, the word of God, which is at work in you who believe. [14]For you, brothers, became imitators of God's churches in Judea, which are in Christ Jesus: You suffered from your own countrymen the same things those churches suffered from the Jews, [15]who killed the Lord Jesus and the prophets and also drove us out. They displease God and are hostile to all men [16]in their effort to keep us from speaking to the Gentiles so that they may be saved. In this way they always heap up their sins to the limit. The wrath of God has come upon them at last.

These verses bring to a graphic climax the thanksgiving that Paul had begun in 1 Thessalonians 1:2. Paul recalls the divided reactions the apostles experienced when they preached the gospel in Thessalonica.

First, *Paul thanks God for the way in which they received God's message* (1 Thess. 2:13): 'You accepted it not as the word of men, but as it actually is, the word of God ...' Because they heard and welcomed the word in this way, it acted to transform their lives.

This is what sets preaching apart from any other form of communication. In James Thompson's words, 'The task of preachers is to confront the congregation with God's own words as they are mediated in scripture.'[23]

And note the present tense in verse 13 – 'which is at work in you'. The gospel is not something heard and embraced only at conversion. The gospel needs to be preached continually to the Church so that it can sustain its ongoing work of shaping lives in conformity to the gospel and creating a faith community. Again in James Thompson's words, 'Without a continuous reminder of the Church's common faith and commitment, the church will never be an authentic community'. So he insists, 'The message to the community of believers involved the re-iteration of the gospel.'[24]

In the sense of a father exhorting his children, Paul never ceased evangelising the Church![25]

Second, *Paul thanks God for the way the gospel made the Thessalonians strong enough to withstand pressure from those who reject God's messengers* (vv.14–16). One particular way in which God's Word in the gospel continues to work in the lives of the Thessalonians is in producing endurance of affliction and suffering.

It is an understatement to say that Paul experienced a fraught relationship with his fellow Jews throughout his mission work, and this passage is one of his harshest reactions to their bitter opposition to his gospel preaching. His words have been taken to be anti-Judaic and sadly have sometimes in the history of the Church been used to justify anti-Semitism. But neither of these two implications need or should be drawn from a closer reading of the text.

Why does Paul commend the Thessalonians for being 'imitators of the churches in Judea' rather than, say, 'in Philippi'?

Because they experienced suffering at the hands of their own countrymen! Just as Jewish Christians in Judea had suffered at the hands of other Jews, so Macedonians are now being persecuted by other Macedonians (Acts 17:5ff.). That Paul mentions how Jewish Christians suffered at the hands of their fellow Jews is deeply ironic since Paul stands on both sides of that equation. Once, as a Jew, he himself inflicted suffering on the Church and now in turn is persecuted by his Jewish opponents!

Paul's criticism of the Judaism he had known and loved is not anti-Semitic but stands in the blunt-speaking tradition both of the prophets and of Jesus Himself, who likewise aroused fierce resentment and hostility from fellow-countrymen that led to martyrdom and crucifixion.

Notice that for Paul to link the sufferings of a predominantly Gentile Christian community with those of the original Judean church serves to underline one of his great passions – that there is only one covenant family of God, made up of both Jews and Greek united in Messiah Jesus!

To say that the sins of Jews who persecute Christian believers have been heaped up 'to the limit' (1 Thess. 2:16b) is tough talking, but Paul's emotional outburst is within the prophetic tradition. His statement that 'The wrath of God has come upon them at last' (v.16c) may refer to a recent famine that had devastated Judea, or may reflect the contemporary upsurge in Zealot militancy and fervour.[26]

Paul's complaint was that they were blocking the path of salvation to the Gentiles and, since this was in contradiction to their own prophetic Scriptures, it was not pleasing to God. If in verse 16c, the literal translation 'unto the end' is a better reading than NIV's 'at last', then Paul is saying that this state of affairs will persist until Christ comes!

When all is said and done this is an area where we need to be ultra-sensitive. Post-Holocaust we should tread warily, lest – heaven forbid – we say or do anything to stir up the anti-Semitism that festers beneath the thin crust of sophistication in the Western world.

But Paul's stark warning must be heard in all its seriousness and pathos if only because it alerts us once more to the fact that the stakes are high, and that eternal outcomes rest on our actions and reactions.

2:17-20

[17]But, brothers, when we were torn away from you for a short time (in person, not in thought), out of our intense longing we made every effort to see you. [18]For we wanted to come to you – certainly I, Paul, did, again and again – but Satan stopped us. [19]For what is our hope, our joy, or the crown in which we will glory in the presence of our Lord Jesus when he comes? Is it not you? [20]Indeed, you are our glory and joy.

The series of images of ministry that included 'infants' (v.7), 'nursing mothers' (v.7), and 'fathers' (v.11) concludes with that of an *orphan* (v.17). Paul confesses that the apostolic band feels 'bereft' or 'orphaned' (*aporphanisthentes*) by being cut off from the Thessalonian Christians. So deep is the bond in the new family of God, for whom baptismal water is thicker than blood.

The use of kinship language throughout the New Testament, as Abraham Malherbe suggests, 'appears to compensate for the natural relationships which were broken or placed under stress' by conversion and resocialisation in the church.[27] But even Paul feels the pain of being torn away from his new family.

Paul recounts his 'intense longing' to see the Thessalonians again. Thwarted in his desire to revisit the church – whether by a specific Satanic action or more likely by a banning order placed on him by the Roman authorities – Paul can bear the strain and anxiety no longer and sends Timothy to get news of the church.

Before we hear his report on the situation, Paul raises the question of the ultimate vindication of all Christian service. So

1 Thessalonians 2:19–20 highlights the issue at stake throughout this letter: *How is success to be measured in an honour–shame culture?*

Paul is able to remind them that he does not seek *praise from men* (1 Thess. 2:6). Paul looks for his vindication to another place and time and to another person altogether. He describes the aims of his ministry in similar vein in verses 12 and 13. Paul conceives it as his fatherly duty so to exhort and instruct as to shape 'lives worthy of God, who calls us into his kingdom and glory'.

That's what we are saved to live for. Set against that ultimate prize, popularity or unpopularity, serenity or suffering along the way eventually matter little. What matters is how by faith we keep our eyes on the goal of glory in the kingdom. We may not make it onto the honours board of this world's empires – Roman or otherwise – but our highest honour is to be found worthy to be in the service of the 'High King of Heaven'. Let that be our vision and Him 'our inheritance now and always'.

For the joy of the kingdom, kingdom people, like their Master, despise the shame and count it an honour to suffer for the sake of the name. It's a pity to miss the glory for the sake of a quiet life. It is this vision of the high and holy future set before us that informs and ennobles all Paul's approaches to ministry. His final evaluation of it is stunning. The crowning glory of his ministry is the Thessalonians (vv.19–20)!

> For what is our hope, our joy, or the crown in which we will glory in the presence of our Lord Jesus when he comes? Is it not you? Indeed, you are our glory and our joy.

Do you see what matters to Paul? Not the interim judgments of people or even the Church, not any honour or applause that comes his way in the meantime. What matters to him is the final valuation when Jesus returns. That's the scope of his perspective.

It's a long-term strategy and a long-range vision, which extends beyond one life span. It invests in people, not things; it sows its life in the soil of self-giving, not self-serving; it focuses not on things that are seen but on the things that are unseen; it reaches beyond the temporal to the eternal. What could be a more attention-grabbing and provocative testimony to Jesus than that, especially in a culture of quick-fix success, instant gratification and short-term everything? What counts is not how things seem now but how well they will look at the Great Arrival on Coronation Day!

3:1-5

¹So when we could stand it no longer, we thought it best to be left by ourselves in Athens. ²We sent Timothy, who is our brother and God's fellow-worker in spreading the gospel of Christ, to strengthen and encourage you in your faith, ³so that no-one would be unsettled by these trials. You know quite well that we were destined for them. ⁴In fact, when we were with you, we kept telling you that we would be persecuted. And it turned out that way, as you well know. ⁵For this reason, when I could stand it no longer, I sent to find out about your faith. I was afraid that in some way the tempter might have tempted you and our efforts might have been useless.

In order to relieve Paul's anxiety, Timothy is dispatched to find out how the Thessalonians are doing (vv.1–5). Paul describes Timothy in heartfelt terms as a 'brother and God's fellow-worker in spreading the gospel of Christ' (v.2).

Timothy was sent to the Thessalonians to strengthen their faith and to encourage them, especially during their trials. These trials and afflictions (*thlipsis*) in which they came to faith have continued, and Paul is anxious that the church is not destabilised.

Forewarned, as we say, is forearmed. Paul could have said, 'I told you so', for he had made clear that such trials were to be expected not only as accidents waiting to happen but also as part of the Church's destiny (vv.3–4). And so it proved to be (v.4b).

It is likely that at this point Paul may have in mind the classic Jewish concept of the Messianic woes, the troubles that were said to attend the followers of the Messiah in the last days (cf Col. 1:24; and the similar idea of 'pains of childbirth' in Rom. 8:22). Had not Jesus Himself said, 'In this world you will have trouble [*thlipsis*]. But take heart! I have overcome the world' (John 16:33)? The idea that Christians will avoid tribulation is preposterous!

Of course, we must distinguish 'affliction/trouble' and 'wrath'. In the New Testament, 'trouble' or 'affliction' always happens to the suffering Church, but 'wrath' never does. 'Wrath' is not our destiny (1 Thess. 5:9) and is what we are saved from by the coming Saviour (1 Thess. 1:10). Wrath is what falls on those who do the afflicting. This affliction is just what authenticates us as genuine followers of the Messiah Jesus!

3:6-10

⁶But Timothy has just now come to us from you and has brought good news about your faith and love. He has told us that you always have pleasant memories of us and that you long to see us, just as we also long to see you. ⁷Therefore, brothers, in all our distress and persecution we were encouraged about you because of your faith. ⁸For now we really live, since you are standing firm in the Lord. ⁹How can we thank God enough for you in return for all the joy we have in the presence of our God because of you? ¹⁰Night and day we pray most earnestly that we may see you again and supply what is lacking in your faith.

There is undeniable relief when Timothy returns to give a favourable report. The tempter has not managed to unsettle the Thessalonian believers, nor have Paul's efforts proved to be futile, as he had been afraid might have been the case (1 Thess. 3:5).

The way in which the Thessalonians are standing firm under pressure now, in turn, encourages Paul and the others in their distress and persecution. Paul can breathe again: 'Knowing that your faith is alive keeps us alive' (v.8, *The Message*). His joy is unsuppressed and quickly overflows in praise (v.9). Now his only concern is to make good the deficiencies in their faith which Timothy's visit has brought to light.

'To supply what is lacking' (v.10) employs the word *katartizo*, which is used in the Gospels of the repairing of nets and so more generally of making good a lack or deficiency.[28] Unable to visit to do this in person, Paul writes this letter which will stand in for his presence and apostolic authority when read aloud in the congregation. What exactly it is that the Thessalonians lack will be made clear from this point on in the letter, and notably in 4:13–18.

Prayer and Reflection

Lord, you are witness to all we are and do.
You are the only audience that really matters.
To live for You and for Your kingdom is all that counts.

Why are we so impressed by the world's view of success, of honour, of shame, of reputation, of prestige?

Thank You, Lord, for the gospel, which is not a man-made recipe for self-improvement but the God-given means of salvation.
Thank You for freeing us through the gospel from society's pressure to conform to its standards of success and achievement.
Thank You, Lord, for teaching us that what matters is not how long we have lived but how deeply we have lived.
Thank You for emboldening us to go against the grain and swim against the tide of fashion.
Keep our eyes focused on the future prize that is coming to us.
Save us from short-term compromise with what has no future in it.
For Yours is the kingdom, the power and the glory,
Amen.

- In the light of Paul's investment in people, reflect on society's current obsession with celebrities and how as Christians we might make true heroes.
- Consider the pressure to conform put upon you, your friends or your children, at work and through popular culture and fashion. How can we as Christians be different without becoming self-righteous?

3:11-4:12 Challenged by His coming

3:11-13

[11]Now may our God and Father himself and our Lord Jesus clear the way for us to come to you. [12]May the Lord make your love increase and overflow for each other and for everyone else, just as ours does for you. [13]May he strengthen your hearts so that you will be blameless and holy in the presence of our God and Father when our Lord Jesus comes with all his holy ones.

Paul's 'prayer wish' here lies at the heart of the letter. It is noteworthy that Paul uses the singular verb (in the optative mood) – 'may he' – so once again bracketing God the Father and Lord Jesus in a way that spotlights almost in passing the remarkably elevated Christology of the earliest faith of the Church.

The prayer also serves to introduce the next two major emphases of the letter – mutual *love* among the believers and personal *holiness* – and both are sharply brought into focus by the prospect of the *parousia*.

So he prays that their *love* may increase and overflow (v. 12; see also 4:9–12), and that they may be found 'blameless and *holy*' (v.13; see also 4:1–8). Paul now proceeds to deal with these ideas in reverse order to the way they appear in the prayer.

4:1-2

[1]Finally, brothers, we instructed you how to live in order to please God, as in fact you are living. Now we ask you and urge you in the Lord Jesus to do this more and more. [2]For you know what instructions we gave you by the authority of the Lord Jesus.

'Finally' is Paul's characteristic starting point for serious talking. This has drawn wry comments from those who observe preachers falling into what they see as bad time-keeping. But this is unfair to Paul. 'Finally' is a poor translation of *loipōn*, which means 'as for the rest', implying 'as for what remains to be said'.

So verses 1 and 2 introduce the whole of Paul's exhortation right down to 5:11. Paul is keen to remind them at every turn of what they already have learned from his teaching (cf 4:1 'we instructed you …'; 4:2 'For you know …'; 4:6 'as we have already told you and warned you …'; 4:9 '… we do not need to write to you'; 4:11 '… just as we told you'; 5:1–2 '… we do not need to write to you, for you know very well …' See also 1:5,8; 2:1,2,5,11; 3:3–4).

Noting this will help to highlight the new teaching he is about to give. It begins at 4:13–18 and is introduced by the telltale phrase 'we do not want you to be ignorant'.

Paul's deeper concern is to rally the Thessalonian Christians to live lives that seek above all to 'please God' in their 'walk' – the usual biblical imagery for the practical business of living. Endeavouring to glorify God by giving him pleasure in every aspect of daily life and behaviour is thus the goal.

4:3–8

[3]It is God's will that you should be sanctified: that you should avoid sexual immorality; [4]that each of you should learn to control his own body in a way that is holy and honourable, [5]not in passionate lust like the heathen, who do not know God; [6]and that in this matter no-one should wrong his brother or take advantage of him. The Lord will punish men for all such sins, as we have already told you and warned you. [7]For God did not call us to be impure, but to live a holy life. [8]Therefore, he who rejects this instruction does not reject man but God, who gives you his Holy Spirit.

'It is God's will that you should be sanctified' (v.3) is the NIV's slight paraphrase, rendered more literally as 'this is the will of God, your sanctification' (NRSV). And Paul's special focus – as we shall see – is sexuality.[29]

A holy God seeks a people whose humanness – as at the beginning – images His character and glory. God called Israel into being to be just that, a people who would be for Him a 'holy nation' (Exod. 19:6). The beating heart of the covenant and Torah that God gave them was the oft-repeated calling: 'be holy because I, the LORD your God, am holy' (Lev. 19:2; etc). It is as if God's call to holiness was meant to pump lifeblood round the veins of the body politic of Israel. It was a vocation intended to mark Israel out from the as-yet-unredeemed pagan nations.

Remarkably Paul reasserts this call to holiness to a church made up of predominantly Gentile believers in Christ. He wants this new church in Thessalonica to stand out from those whom he says 'do not know God' (1 Thess. 4:5c). To know God – this holy and distinctive God – is to reflect his character in your own distinctive and holy behaviour.

With this in mind, Paul employs the full range of holiness language to drive the message home. So words from the *hagiaos* root abound.

- God's will is our *hagiasmos* – perhaps implying the process of sanctification, of being made holy.
- Especially is this to be shown in the area of sexual conduct so that we act (v.4) in *hagiasmō* – in holiness, in a holy way.
- For God has not called us (v.7) to uncleanness but to *hagiasmō* with the great responsibility (v.8) of accepting or rejecting God's *to pneuma autou to hagion* – His own *Holy* Spirit!

Biblically, we recall, *holiness is God's essential nature*. It stresses His otherness. His being holy is what makes Him utterly distinctive and sets Him apart from all else as God in His majestic moral purity.

So for us holiness implies *separateness*, being set aside for God's exclusive cause. To be holy is to be as distinctive in our own way as God is in His. It is to dare as God's holy people to be as different as God, to stand out as belonging to Him by our purity and goodness in a sinful society and a corrupt culture.

This high, holy, God-pleasing calling is the only true path to self-expression and self-fulfilment because it is what we were made and redeemed for. Our becoming holy like Him is the only way for us to be happy like Him. But try applying that to human sexual behaviour! What could be more countercultural than this? However, it was no less so in Thessalonica when Paul first said it.

- The *Graeco-Roman world* tolerated sexual laxity and extreme sexual permissiveness. Taking a mistress, frequenting brothels, using prostitutes – these were all positively encouraged and regarded as normal behaviour. 'Innkeepers and owners of cookshops frequently kept slave-girls for the sexual entertainment of their customers.'[30] The classic Judaeo-Christian view of all this is that it is utter perversion. But the great orator Demosthenes celebrated such perversion: 'Concubines for daily needs, mistresses for pleasure (that is a courtesan or lover known and approved by one's wife) and wives to bear us legitimate children'! A very male view of the matter, you notice – though it's tragic to see how modern feminism in the quest for a spurious freedom has scrambled so hard to get its slice of this particularly toxic cake.
- The *religious cults* popular in Thessalonica also promoted sexual activity as part of their practice. Strong phallic symbolism was associated with the cults of Dionysus, Cabirus and Samothrace.

Thessalonica was a *sex-saturated society* – much like the modern Western world. It was in breaking with this contemporary idolatry that the converts faced their sharpest initial challenge. But the pressure to conform never relented and the 'affliction' they endured was no doubt the cost of their ongoing struggle to stay pure and be different.

Now as then, the more tolerant, permissive and 'free' a culture professes to be, the less it tolerates those who stand apart from its values and mores, and stand out as a distinctive group.

Christians are committed to doing God's will as the way to their own happiness and fulfilment, and Paul spells out in detail how this applies to our sexual behaviour in three ways, each introduced in English translations of his letter with the word 'that'.

God's will in willing our sanctification is: '*that you should avoid sexual immorality*' (v.3b). 'Sexual immorality' translates the word *porneia*, which is here used of all sexual activity outside of marriage. Avoiding this was no doubt regarded as strange and scandalous in the ancient world; as it is today.

Our culture is very like that of the first-century Graeco-Roman world. In both, sexuality is completely divorced from morality. But Paul is absolutely clear on this. In Gordon Fee's passionate words, 'You cannot have sex with someone outside of marriage and love that person at the same time!'[31]

Thomas Howard wonderfully captures the preciousness of God's gift of sexuality in his lovely little book, *Hallowed be this House*. In it he reflects on all the rooms in a house and how they mirror the presence and joy of God in our lives. To do so Howard uses priestly and holiness language. He likens the bedroom to the 'holy of holies'. The bedroom, he says, is a sacred place where we are most likely to be conceived and where often we die. The way babies are made illustrates the sacredness.

> My life laid down for you; our two lives laid down, becoming one life, and in this laying down and union, lo, the springing forth of new life. My service to you turning out to be joy. Your life laid down for me turning out to be joy. Your acceptance of me being itself your gift to me.

But as with every sacred place, he continues, taboos attach to this union. Listen to him:

> One of the taboos, for example, has been that complete sexual union does not rightly occur outside the bonds of fidelity. 'Forsaking all other', says the Christian marriage rite. The idea is that the man and the woman keep themselves exclusively for each other, at least on this level of things.

> Why? Is their union some privileged society that discriminates against all the rest of us? Well, yes, in a word. It is privileged and it does discriminate. The only one who had the privilege of entering that particular shrine (the body of the other) is the priest who has pledged his faithfulness to that shrine alone.
> We can't all share that privilege, reiterates Howard. 'The rite is a privileged one, reserved exclusively for the one priest who has pledged himself to faithful attendance on this shrine.'[32]

God's will in willing our sanctification and holiness is: '*that each of you should learn how to control his own body in a way that is holy and honourable*' (v.4). The NIV is on the right lines, I think, in opting to translate an unusual Greek word as 'body'. The word is *skeous* which often means 'vessel' or 'pot' (as in Rom. 9:21–23).

It has to do in this context with human bodily functions so 'body', as we said, is on the right lines. But it needs to be made even more specific to fit Paul's case. I have no doubt that Paul is doing some plain talking here, which is better represented by translating: 'You should learn to gain control of your genitals'![33] That the reference is to the male sex organ receives support from the use of *skeous* in the Greek Old Testament at 1 Samuel 21:5b: 'Men's things [genitalia] are holy even on missions that are not holy.' Learn to control your own sex drive in a way that is honourable and holy and 'not in passionate lust like the heathen' (1 Thess. 4:5a).

Sexuality is a gift to be bestowed in the right place and at the right time. It is not to be thrown around at whim – 'putting it about' as the pathetic jargon has it – in fits of rampant lust. It is not to be indulged in because two people 'have the hots' for each other – to use again the flippant and dreadful jargon – for it is not given as an excuse for discharge of an over-heated animal passion.

Reducing sex to testosterone and hormones – that is what the pagans do. Pre-marital and extra-marital sex is a pagan practice, normal only for those who 'do not know God', an aberration to those who do know Him! And as Wendell Berry says about abortion on demand: self-control not surgery is the answer.

Third, *'that in this matter no-one should wrong his brother or take advantage of him'* (v.6) – alongside 'brother' read 'sister' for Paul intends to be gender-inclusive here. It is unthinkable, he argues, that this should be going on *within* the church family.

Christians have every reason for pleasing God by keeping sexually pure. Paul mentions *three good reasons* for doing so.

1. Because of future judgment by the Lord Jesus who is protective of His Body, the Church. 'The Lord will punish men for all such sins, as we have already told you and warned you' (v.6b). The threat of the Lord's disfavour and punishment should deter even the possibility, and the fear of the Lord should dispel it altogether. Holy love and loving self-control show respect in the family of God.

2. Because of the past call of God's on our lives to be God's holy people, called to reflect His character as a pure and holy God. 'For God did not call us to be impure, but to live a holy life' (v.7).

3. Above all and most remarkably, we can be sexually pure because of the present gift of the Holy Spirit to us – and to do otherwise is to reject His work in our lives. 'Therefore, he who rejects this instruction does not reject man but God, who gives you his Holy Spirit' (v.8). The verb 'gives' is in the present tense, reminding us that the Spirit is continuously working in us to empower us to be

holy. No one can claim to be powerless in face of temptation or say, 'I can't help myself.'

Paul is here directly and vividly drawing on the prophetic promises of the new covenant made by God at the time of the Exile and made good for us by the death of Jesus and the gift of the Spirit.[34] In particular Paul has in mind Ezekiel 36:25–27: 'I will sprinkle clean water on you, and you will be clean; I will cleanse you from all your impurities and from all your idols' – even if sexual impurity is part of your idolatrous cultural baggage it's what you have been converted from (1 Thess. 1:9–10); 'I will give you a new heart and put a new spirit in you; I will remove from you your heart of stone and give you a heart of flesh. And I will put my Spirit in you and move you to … keep my laws.'

The promise is repeated in Ezekiel 37:6,14 where the phrase is 'I will put breath/my Spirit *in* [or *into*] you'. This explains the rather odd but quite deliberate way in which Paul writes of 'God who *gives* the Holy Spirit *into* you' (*eis humas*, 1 Thess. 4:8). This is a deliberate echo of the Greek Old Testament at Ezekiel 37:6,14. So even by his careful choice of language, Paul is reminding the Thessalonians that they have entered into the joy and power of the realities of the new covenant.

To flaunt a supposed sexual freedom in the face of such clear apostolic teaching at this point is to defy God and to reject the reality of the Spirit in our life, however charismatic we may claim to be. On the other hand, how wonderful that erstwhile pagans, now believers in Jesus, are now included by grace and faith in the one covenant family of God and bear the identity marker of the Holy Spirit to prove it.

Holiness is possible, sexual purity is possible. Christians are not at the mercy of an oppressive culture; it is not inevitable that our young people succumb to the crushing pressure of the media or the lies peddled by the entertainment and pop industries. Christians are filled with the empowering Holy Spirit of the Holy God and can be different if they dare to be different.

How do we communicate this vision even to our own Christian young people in our modern pagan culture? It is not, insists Gordon Fee, that God is hung-up about sex; we are! God is pro-creation. He thinks it's all good, the two-people-one-flesh in intimacy and joy is His gift.

Listen to Fee's wise and strong words:

> I am weary of a culture that has adopted a pagan view of freedom and has taken this precious gift of the Creator God and trashed it and then used it to sell every last thing that is to be sold by a degraded sexuality ... and that still thinks it's free! Our culture is enslaved to its sexuality.[35]

Can the church show a different way? Please God, it can! This has little to do with rules and regulations and nothing remotely to do with being traditional or old-fashioned. This is all about living the way God intended us to live in His image. This is all about living as part of His new creation in the power of His Holy Spirit with new covenant consequences that give glory to God and startle a satiated and bored world.

So God, holiness and genitalia are connected!

Summary

Pleasing God by sexual purity is called for by God's character. Sexual purity is about knowing God and knowing what kind of God He is, and reflecting something of that radiant, radical holiness and passionate purity in one's sexuality by the grace of the Spirit of holiness Himself.

Sexual purity?

- God's will demands it (1 Thess. 4:3)
- God's family deserves it (1 Thess. 4:6)
- God's calling evokes it (1 Thess. 4:7)
- God's Spirit enables it (1 Thess. 4:8).

4:9-12

⁹Now about brotherly love we do not need to write to you, for you yourselves have been taught by God to love each other. ¹⁰And in fact, you do love all the brothers throughout Macedonia. Yet we urge you, brothers, to do so more and more.

¹¹Make it your ambition to lead a quiet life, to mind your own business and to work with your hands, just as we told you, ¹²so that your daily life may win the respect of outsiders and so that you will not be dependent on anybody.

Love for sisters and brothers in the family of God reinforces the call to holiness. No one fights this battle alone. We are family. We have been lovingly embedded in an embodied life-support system.

- God teaches us His kind of love in word and deed. Here too is an echo of the new covenant as promised by Isaiah (Isa. 54:13). God models this love in the stooping of His Son to wash dusty feet and in the giving of His life for us, even to the death of the cross.
- We can't teach God any lessons in love; we've learnt it all from Him. Herein is love: not that we loved God and set a precedent for Him, but that He loved us and sent His Son to be the propitiation for our sins, so showering us with love and showing us how to do it.
- Paul urges the Thessalonians and us to go on loving, only more so.

So Paul urges his readers to live responsibly (vv.11–12). Get on with your work to the glory of God. Paul's example in this won him respect and proved his credibility (1 Thess. 2:9; cf 2 Thess. 3:7–10).

Living a quiet life need not be unadventurous as long as you think of yourselves as spies sent out into enemy territory, subversives planting explosive charges of truth, love and good deeds behind enemy lines. But if we do take to the streets let us do so in the servant spirit of Him who did not raise His voice raucously in the streets as some crazed rabble-rouser, who did not parade His piety or seek to enforce His will, even by strength of personality. So let our protests be peaceful and our resistance non-violent. Love our enemies to death – and wait for the fireworks to start!

Live modestly and discreetly; live dangerously and differently. Live distinctively, reflecting the character of God – not 'like the heathen, who do not know God' (1 Thess. 4:5; cf 4:13; 5:4,6) but as those who seek to please the God they know and love. So may our hearts be strengthened by God's Word and the Spirit, that we may be part of the answer to Paul's prayer and so be found 'blameless and holy in the presence of our God and Father when our Lord Jesus comes with all his holy ones' (1 Thess. 3:13).

Prayer and Reflection

You, Lord, are the Wholly Other.
Only You can make goodness attractive to us, for our moral sense has been corrupted by sin.
Without You we love darkness rather than light.

With You we begin to discern that everything is sacred and all of life is a sacrament of grace.

We realise now we handle *holy things*:
bread and wine, basins and towels, money and sex, at work and play, in bedrooms and boardrooms.
In all these things, hallowed be your name.

We realise afresh that we are marked as *holy people*,
hallowed by Your call, consecrated by Your loving claim on our lives.

We remember – though less often than we might – that we walk on *holy ground*, hallowed by the blood You shed on this earth.

So fill us with the Holy Spirit that we may enjoy a holy and hilarious sexuality, embody a holy and passionate servanthood, and be inspired to a holy and extravagant creativity.
May these signs of new creation be like springtime for the world.

Everything we know about love, You have taught us,
    in unwearying faithfulness,
    in unforgettable example,
    in unspeakable suffering.
By Your cross and Holy Spirit make and keep us holy.

- Consider ways in which the Christian use of sexuality might be a strikingly countercultural sign of the kingdom to a sex-saturated society.
- Our happiness and God's holiness coincide; do you really believe it?

4:13–18 Comforted by His coming

[13]Brothers, we do not want you to be ignorant about those who fall asleep, or to grieve like the rest of men, who have no hope. [14]We believe that Jesus died and rose again and so we believe that God will bring with Jesus those who have fallen asleep in him. [15]According to the Lord's own word, we tell you that we who are still alive, who are left till the coming of the Lord, will certainly not precede those who have fallen asleep. [16]For the Lord himself will come down from heaven, with a loud command, with the voice of the archangel and with the trumpet call of God, and the dead in Christ will rise first. [17]After that, we who are still alive and are left will be caught up together with them in the clouds to meet the Lord in the air. And so we will be with the Lord for ever. [18]Therefore encourage each other with these words.

When Eric Wolterstorff was killed at the age of 25 in a climbing accident in the Alps, his father, the distinguished Christian Professor of Philosophical Theology at Yale, Nicholas Wolterstorff, gave vent to his grief in what has become a classic: *Lament for a Son*.

He wrote

Elements of the gospel which I had always thought would console me did not … It did not console me to be reminded of the hope of resurrection. If I had forgotten that hope, then it would indeed have brought light into my life to be reminded of it. But I did not think of death as a bottomless pit. I did not grieve as one who has no hope. Yet Eric is gone, *here* and *now* he is gone; *now* I cannot talk with him, *now* I cannot see him, *now* I cannot hug him, *now* I cannot hear his plans for the future. *That* is my sorrow. A friend said; 'He's in good hands'. I was deeply moved. But that reality does not put Eric back in my hands now. That's my grief. For that grief, what consolation can there be than having him back?[36]

Writing letters of condolence to the recently bereaved is always a tricky art. How well Irene did, I leave you to judge. She wrote somewhere in the ancient world, sometime in the first century:

Irene, to Taonnophris and Philo good comfort.
I am sorry and weep over the departed one as I wept for Didymas. And I have done everything that was appropriate as have all of my family, Epaphroditus and Thermuthian and Philion and Apollonius and Plantas. But even so, against such things there is nothing anyone can do. So comfort each other. May you be well.[37]

Notice the haunting words: 'there is nothing anyone can do' – just one small sample of the widespread and near total despair over death in the ancient world.

Paul, apostle of Jesus who died and rose again, is sure that there is something that Someone has done and will do that makes a difference to death. In his first Epistle to the Thessalonians, Paul is writing a letter of condolence to console those in the Thessalonian church whose loved ones and fellow-believers have died. In effect, Paul is moved to say something to them which will answer the questions of the newly bereaved and give them hope and comfort. Their questions have arisen because of the conviction formed in them by Paul's teaching that Jesus will return. This is the first fact to be reckoned with – the *return of Jesus, His* parousia.

The term *parousia* is one Paul borrowed from the political vocabulary of the Roman Empire. As we have noted before, *parousia* was a technical term in imperial imagery used of the visit of a very important person – a leading dignitary, the governor or even the emperor on a state visit – which was attended by huge pomp and ceremony.

But the apostles declared the impending 'state visit' not of a VIP but of the MIP – The Most Important Person – whose Great Arrival would trump all other grand entrances and whose glory would eclipse all other regality. No wonder the Caesars got jumpy when this message started taking hold in the key cities of their empire. One of the edicts that Paul and Silas probably infringed in Thessalonica was an imperial order banning the predictions of a another ruler who would upstage and displace the emperor.

More immediately this prospect raised a pastoral issue for Paul in his relationships with the Thessalonians. Their anxious question is simply this: *What happens to those who die in Christ before the Lord's return?* How will they stand at the *parousia*?

Now that is the key to this section of the letter, and in fact the only question Paul is answering in it. He is not giving details about the chronology of the last times or about the sequence of events leading up to the coming of Jesus. Whatever some may believe, Paul is emphatically not furnishing them with insider knowledge on some secret rapture of the Church. It is not even his intention to do so. That is not his concern at all.

His one concern is to bring consolation to those wondering about the fate of the Christian dead. His focus is on the status and destiny of those who – as he puts it – 'fall asleep' (v.13). By employing this metaphor, he is not implying anything that might give rise to any kind of erroneous teaching about 'soul sleep'. He is simply using a common euphemism for death. Those who 'have fallen asleep in him' (vv.14 and 15) are the 'dead in Christ' (v.16). These are twice contrasted with 'we who are still alive' (15a) and 'are left' (v.15b). It is the living who have been 'left behind' by the dead; that is, the Christians who remain alive at Christ's return.

What some in the Thessalonian church are wondering is whether, when Jesus returns, the living will have an advantage over the dead in Christ. To answer this is Paul's aim. Let's see how he goes about it.

Paul has taught them about the Lord's return and about the resurrection but now he is imparting new information to the Thessalonian Christians. The sure indicator for this is a phrase he uses elsewhere when he is telling his readers something he has not taught them before: 'We do not want you to be ignorant about ...' (v.13a).

He understands their grief and no doubt feels with them. But he urges them in their sorrow not to grieve as those who have no hope (v.13b). Praise God, like the rest of humanity we grieve over our loss, but even Christian grief is different from any other.

The next move in his exhortation – in verse 14a – is to recall another aspect of what they already know and believe: *the resurrection of Jesus Christ from the dead – which by implication guarantees that believers too will be raised from the dead.*

But the way Paul describes this here offers a hopeful new dimension to their faith (v.14b): When God brings back to our world the Risen Christ, He 'will bring with Jesus those who have fallen asleep'. This is part of the new information spelt out to answer the anxiety of the grieving Thessalonian believers.

More specifically still (v.15) – in answering their concern – Paul makes it absolutely clear that those who have died in Christ will not be at any disadvantage compared to those believers who remain alive: 'According to the Lord's own word, we tell you that we who are still alive, who are left till the coming of the Lord, will *certainly not precede* those who have fallen asleep' (emphasis added).

Notice by the way that Paul refers to this new information as 'according to the Lord's own word' (v.15). It's not clear what he means by this. He could be referring to a prophetic word through him from the Risen Christ, which is unlikely since Paul elsewhere makes this clear when it happens (eg 1 Cor. 7:10–12). It could mean a statement of Jesus not recorded in the Gospels (as Acts 20:35) or perhaps lost to us. More likely it is Paul's way of saying that he is summarising teaching that Jesus gave about the matter.

Then he gives the reason for his confidence, in verses 16 and 17:

For the Lord himself will come down from heaven, with a loud command, with the voice of the archangel and with the trumpet call of God, and the dead in Christ will rise first. After that, we who are still alive and are left will be caught up together with them in the clouds to meet the Lord in the air. And so we will be with the Lord for ever.

Now here is Paul's teaching on the so-called *rapture*. What can we make of it? Well, certainly not as much as some do who write speculative, glossy-covered, bestselling books on the subject!

First of all, the scenario of a 'rapture' – which so fascinates, indeed obsesses, many evangelical Christians – is couched in pictorial language that must not – repeat *not* – be taken with strict literalism. The terminology is classic imagery familiar to readers of Jewish apocalyptic writings and biblical prophets, such as the book of Daniel.

The divine command that has the last word on history, the archangelic voice, the last trumpet to gather God's people, the air as the site of spiritual powers, and the clouds as signifying God's majestic presence – these are all stock biblical images. They are not less real for being figurative, but more real.

But this is language at the edge of meaning. We are here trying to describe the indescribable, for which there is no precedent. The only language we can employ to depict things that are not yet in existence is the language we use to describe what is here already. Crassly literal minds can make hay with speculation here – if you'll excuse the pun – but end up in nonsense.

So what of the 'rapture'? The word 'rapture' is merely from the Latinised form, *rapio*, of the Greek word used here by Paul for 'caught up' (v.17). The word in Greek, 'harpagēsometha', means simply 'snatched' or 'seized' – without in itself having any connotation of 'up'.

Furthermore the spatial directions taken so literalistically by some are decidedly shaky. The pop-prophecy books tend to insert into the exegesis here their interpretation of Matthew 24:36–41. There Jesus says that no one knows about the day or the hour, not the angels, not even Him (so perhaps Hal Lindsay knows better than Jesus?) – only the Father.

But when the day comes, it will be like the days of Noah in catching a self-absorbed generation by surprise. So, says Jesus, 'Two men will be in the field; one will be taken and the other left.

Two women will be grinding with a hand mill; one will be taken and the other left.' Again some make a great deal of those being taken and being left. They confidently assume that the ones being taken are the ones being saved, while the ones left behind are lost. But this is a precarious assumption at best. In fact, exegetically, the reverse could just as well be true. In context, Jesus speaks of those who 'knew nothing about what would happen until the flood came and *took them all away*' (Matt. 24:39) – where 'being taken way' means 'taken away in judgment'.

And what of a *secret* rapture? The text hardly portrays a secret rapture of the Church, which passes unnoticed by the world at large. I imagine you've heard the usual nonsense about two people on a tandem and the one at the front, finding the going getting tough, looks round only to find his Christian friend has disappeared – allegedly having been raptured!

But a secret event? Listen to it. A loud command, the voice of the archangel, a trumpet blast … it doesn't sound like a secret event to me.

What about the directions involved? Well, if anyone should want to play silly spatio-geographical games, in which direction are we supposed to be going? The dead in Christ are coming with Him – presumably, if you insist on it, downwards – while at the same time they are rising from the grave, presumably upwards! By this time I'm not sure who's coming or going.

And if you still insist on taking all this literally, rather than figuratively as you should, it's worth pointing out what the rare word used for 'meeting' implies. The word *apentesis* is used in only two other places in the New Testament. Both are interesting.

It is a technical word, also found in secular Greek, to describe a delegation of townspeople who go out to meet a visiting dignitary and – this is the point – return with him whence they came in the direction he was moving in. So, perhaps even more significantly (was it in Paul's mind?) the word occurs in the parable of the virgins in Matthew 25:1,6. Similarly, it is used in Acts 28:15 where Luke pictures a group of believers coming out of Rome to meet up with Paul on the Appian Way and escort him back into the city.

If all this did not bear so much on what is common but – in my view – erroneous teaching, we would begrudge the time we spent on this. For it nearly misses the entire point of the glorious, wonderful, hope-filled message Paul is offering here.

Let's celebrate the central message of this passage. Our blessed Lord Jesus, who died to save us from final wrath, is coming back again. When He comes, the dead in Christ will rise first, we shall all gain brand new resurrection bodies and – the bit the Thessalonians must have rejoiced to hear – we, together with them, will meet Him and be with Him together for ever. Together with them!

Resurrection is a staggering possibility we scarcely dare dream of. But *reunion* – that is, if anything, what lies closest to our hearts as what we deeply long for. To be together with them, our loved ones in Christ who have gone to be with the Lord, to meet them again – that surely is what the recently bereaved Thessalonians, and long-bereaved Nicholas Wolterstorff, and you and I want above all.

After all, what was the first thing Jesus did following his own resurrection? He went to meet his disciples. In Austin Farrer's words, 'He was the first to die of the divine fellowship. Since none of his human friends were in heaven, no wonder if he came to find them on earth.'[38]

Henry Alford celebrated the great reunion at the Great Arrival with a hopelessly jumbled mixture of apocalyptic images, but who's counting?

Ten thousand times ten thousand,
In sparkling raiment bright,
The armies of the ransomed saints
Throng up the steeps of light:

O then what raptured greetings
On Canaan's happy shore,

What knitting severed friendships up,
Where partings are no more!
Then eyes with joy shall sparkle
That brimmed with tears of late;
Orphans no longer fatherless,
Nor widows desolate.

And that's language fit to burst its seams. It's all going to be infinitely better than that! Above all, we have the promise that is better than anything: 'And so we will be with the Lord for ever' (1 Thess. 4:17b). What could be better than that?

All that Paul teaches here he insists is to enable us to 'encourage each other with these words' (v.18). We grieve but not as the pagans do. Says Nicholas Wolterstorff at one stage of his grief:

The Stoics of antiquity said; Be calm. Disengage yourself. Neither laugh nor weep. Jesus says; be open to the wounds of the world. Mourn humanity's mourning, weep over humanity's weeping, be wounded by humanity's wounds, be in agony over humanity's agony. But do so in the good cheer that the day of peace is coming.[39]

Why do evangelicals use up so much energy contesting, combating and contradicting each other with these words, rather than comforting one another with them? Maybe if we stopped fighting over Jesus' *second* coming the world might hear the good news of His *first* coming more readily.

Nicholas Wolterstorff jotted this down one day in his lament for Eric:

I shall try to keep the wound from healing, in recognition of our living still in the old order of things. I shall try to keep it from healing, in solidarity with those who sit beside me on humanity's mourning bench.[40]

Let's nourish ourselves with the comfort and hope that Paul's breathtaking vision offers us. Then we might have enough comfort left over for those who have yet to come to faith – and find courage and strength, as Nicholas Wolterstorff puts it, to sit on 'humanity's mourning bench' with them. Perhaps by our very presence we may enable them to catch through blurred eyes a glimpse of the gospel of hope.

Prayer and Reflection

Without them ...
Without those we loved and were loved by ...
   ... the mourning bench of bereavement is always crowded,
   ... there is a black hole in our hearts,
   ... old scars in our history of love still ache in cold climates,
   ... 'empty chairs and empty tables' tell their own tale of
   dashed hopes and broken dreams.

With You ...
Is it possible that even death takes on a strange turn?
Is it possible to grieve still but to grieve differently?
Is it possible to 'rage against the dying of the light' and find
strange comfort?
With You, all things, even these, are possible.

Where are they, those we have loved?
Where have they gone, those who loved us?
Are they *with You*?

Heaven will not be heaven without You or without them!
So shall we be together, and together, be with the Lord!
   redemption ...
   resurrection ...
   reunion ...
These words give us a new song to sing. We relish the realities
they represent.
With these words we comfort one another
So may 'the music of thy name refresh my soul in death'.
Amen.

Pause to give thanks for the memory of all your loved ones who
have died in Christ. Reflect on how Paul's teaching informs and
inspires Christian hope.

5:1-11 Confounded by His coming

5:1-3

> ¹Now, brothers, about times and dates we do not need to write to you, ²for you know very well that the day of the Lord will come like a thief in the night. ³While people are saying, 'Peace and safety', destruction will come on them suddenly, as labour pains on a pregnant woman, and they will not escape.

Having discharged his burden of giving them new teaching in the exhortation of 4:13–18, Paul can now remind the Thessalonians of things that they already know about the future and about living in its light.

Again Paul passes over the *timing* of the final events. But whatever he can assume to have previously taught the Thessalonians, it does not need repeating or elaborating upon. So often Paul's concerns are very different from modern preoccupations and obsessions. Our curiosity may excite us but we're not going to get answers to many things either the apostles themselves didn't know or don't deem important enough to mention. Infuriating, isn't it? But there it is. We would do well to be the ones doing the adjusting at this point and rejoicing in what as been revealed to us.

Paul uses two graphic images to capture how the Day of the Lord comes. It will come:

- suddenly and unexpectedly – like a thief in the night;
- suddenly and unavoidably – like labour pains.

A word about the second image first: 'While people are saying, "Peace and safety", destruction will come on them suddenly, as labour pains on a pregnant woman, and they will not escape' (v.3). There is clear Old Testament background to such language.

Jeremiah rails against a false peace and complacency (Jer. 6:14; cf Ezek. 13:10), which Isaiah says can be instantly shattered (Isa. 29:5–6; 47:9). Isaiah specifically uses the image of labour pains to illustrate the suddenness of such judgment (Isa. 13:8–9).

As an apostle, Paul is speaking with prophetic authority a word from Israel's God, the One Creator who is sovereign over history and nations. But the political context in which Paul is writing must surely also be in his mind. The slogan 'peace and safety' sounds exactly like a piece of typical imperial propaganda thought up by the spin-doctors in Rome. The Roman Empire – like all human empires – was really a glorified and efficient protection racket.

Rome guaranteed law, order and peace to its subjugated peoples under the shadow of Roman military power and by exacting heavy taxes and tribute to pay for the privilege. It was all undergirded by the spreading cult of offering homage and worship to the emperor, which the Caesars did nothing to discourage. This was the vaunted 'peace of Rome', characterising an imperial order that seemed impregnable and immoveable.

But come the Day of the Lord, and the roof will fall in on all such empires. That final day will only make clear what has been true all along: that sovereignty belongs only to God and to His Christ – our Lord, Jesus Christ. In that conviction, Paul can boldly reassure the tiny church in one of Rome's more important outposts that – as Richard Horsley puts it – 'history was running not through but against Rome'.[41]

Sure enough – though beyond Paul's lifespan – the final curtain fell on the glory of the 'eternal city' and its worldwide rule, and one day it will curtail all the proud human empires still holding sway. Now, as then, only those who have found peace with God through the cross of Jesus will be secure in a future guaranteed by His resurrection.

We can see how this section of the letter differs from 4:13–18. There Paul focuses on the *parousia*; here on the 'Day of the Lord'. He is speaking of course of the same reality. But *parousia* is believers' language, used in contexts such as 1 Thessalonians 4:13–18 where Christians are being comforted by the prospect of the Lord's return.

'Day of the Lord' language, on the other hand, as used here, addresses unbelievers as well as believers and comes with heavier portent. It portends judgment as well as grace. It is a day that does not necessarily bring light but darkness (Amos 5:18–20; Joel 1:15; Isa. 13:6–9).

Whereas *parousia* is associated with gathering, the 'Day of the Lord' brings division. Whereas *parousia* evokes images of reunion, 'the Day of the Lord' speaks of separation.

So now Paul develops the first image he had employed in mentioning the coming Day of the Lord; that of *the thief in the night*. Here he can draw directly on the Jesus tradition (Matt. 24:33; Luke 12:39): 'for you know very well that the day of the Lord will come like a thief in the night' (1 Thess. 5:2). It needs to be said that this image never implies 'soonness' but 'suddenness'; and in particular unexpectedness, which catches sinners unawares.

5:4–11

[4]But you, brothers, are not in darkness so that this day should surprise you like a thief. [5]You are all sons of the light and sons of the day. We do not belong to the night or to the darkness. [6]So then, let us not be like others, who are asleep, but let us be alert and self-controlled. [7]For those who sleep, sleep at night, and those who get drunk, get drunk at night. [8]But since we belong to the day, let us be self-controlled, putting on faith and love as a breastplate, and the hope of salvation as a helmet. [9]For God did not appoint us to suffer wrath but to receive salvation through our Lord Jesus Christ. [10]He died for us so that, whether we are awake or asleep, we may live together with him. [11]Therefore encourage one another and build each other up, just as in fact you are doing.

Paul immediately makes a clear distinction between believers and unbelievers over this. 'But you ... are not in darkness so that this day should surprise you like a thief. You are all sons of the light and sons of the day' (vv.4–5a). You are not in the dark over this. You live your lives in the light of God's revelation and love; you need not therefore be surprised when the day unexpectedly arrives. But you should be people who are always keenly alert, whose spiritual and mental senses are not befuddled like those of a drunkard (vv.6–7).

Because of who you are, you remain vigilant. You do not get so immersed in the routine business of making a living and raising a family that you never give heed to bigger issues, to transcendent facts, to future destiny. Such people are 'asleep' – Paul here confusingly changes the use of this metaphor from 4:13 where it means 'death' to its meaning here of those whose careless indifference and eyes-down materialism causes them, like Rip van Winkle, to 'sleep through a revolution'.

No, you are the sons of the day. Stay awake to the reality of heaven and hell, of God's coming and kingdom, so that when that day comes you will *not be caught out by it but caught up in it.*

Christians, you have a different story, a different history and a different destiny. Act like it, behave like it, think like it, hope like it, rejoice like it ... and dress like it! 'Since we belong to the day, let us be self-controlled, putting on faith and love as a breastplate, and the hope of salvation as a helmet' (v.8). Again we clothe ourselves with the familiar triad of virtues for which the Thessalonians had already become noted (1 Thess. 1:2–3).

The military imagery recalls the prophetic vision of God as Warrior in Isaiah 59:15–17. It anticipates Paul's words to the Romans: 'The night is nearly over; the day is almost here. So let us put aside the deeds of darkness and put on the armour of light' (Rom. 13:12). So we can see from 1 Thessalonians 5:4–8 how different are:

'Darkness people' from	'Daylight people'
night (v.5) darkness (vv.4,5) sleep (vv.6–7) drunken (v.7)	sons of day (v.5) sons of light (v.5) awake, alert (v.6) sober (vv.6,8)

The kind of people we are and the stance we adopt reflects which kingdom we belong to and the prospects we share in belonging to it.

Rome's spurious peace gives way to God's permanent peace. Its false security (v.3) fades into nothing in the light of complete final salvation (vv.9–10). The prospects for Rome and for a faith that trusts all such fragile peace and stability are sudden destruction and crushing disillusionment. But we have:

> turned to God from idols to serve the living and true God, and to wait for his Son from heaven ... who rescues us from the coming wrath ... For God did not appoint us to suffer wrath but to receive salvation through our Lord Jesus Christ. He died for us so that, whether we are awake or asleep, we may live together with him. (1 Thess. 1:9–10; 5:9–10)

Let us *encourage* one another with these realities. Let us build up the Church – not divide the Church – with this stunning outlook and glorious hope.

Prayer and Reflection

Lord, in our apocalyptic world, we need Your wisdom and courage.

We know that the only true sequel to the tragedy of the twin towers is the 'return of the King'.

We know too that militarism, technology, affluence will not save us when the roof caves in on our vaunted Western way of life.

Deep down, we know this but ...

... still we opt for the 'peace and security' the empire offers us,

... still we blunder about as if we were in the dark about ultimate realities.

We confess to being anxious and fearful; anxious about our old age or worried about what will happen to our children.

Train us in the new way of Your kingdom to trust in Your future.

Talk us into walking by faith towards the oncoming Christ, for He alone is the light at the end of history's long tunnel.

Even so, come, Lord Jesus.

Amen.

- How might the vision of the future in this chapter affect the way you live your daily life?
- How best can the Church bear witness to God's future in a world which offers false 'peace and security'?

5:12-28 Completed at His coming

5:12-24

¹²Now we ask you, brothers, to respect those who work hard among you, who are over you in the Lord and who admonish you. ¹³Hold them in the highest regard in love because of their work. Live in peace with each other. ¹⁴And we urge you, brothers, warn those who are idle, encourage the timid, help the weak, be patient with everyone. ¹⁵Make sure that nobody pays back wrong for wrong, but always try to be kind to each other and to everyone else.

¹⁶Be joyful always; ¹⁷pray continually; ¹⁸give thanks in all circumstances, for this is God's will for you in Christ Jesus.

¹⁹Do not put out the Spirit's fire; ²⁰ do not treat pophecies with contempt. ²¹Test everything. Hold on to the good. ²²Avoid every kind of evil.

²³May God himself, the God of peace, sanctify you through and through. May your whole spirit, soul and body be kept blameless at the coming of our Lord Jesus Christ. ²⁴The one who calls you is faithful and he will do it.

We start at the end of this section with the key prayer wish (v.23) in which Paul prays for wholeness and completeness at His *parousia*. This is appropriate, for the point Paul has been making throughout the letter is that as Christians we live our lives out of the hope and energy generated by the End to which we are moving. 'May God himself, the God of peace, sanctify you through and through ['wholly' or 'entirely']. May your whole spirit, soul and body be kept blameless at the coming of our Lord Jesus Christ' (v.23).

Let's not get hung up on biblical psychology – whether or not Paul is advocating a tripartite view of human personality. That is not the point of the prayer. The emphasis falls on precisely the opposite – on the wholeness and completeness of what is to happen to the whole person.

So let's hear it again with that emphasis in mind: 'May God himself, the God of peace, sanctify you *through and through* *['wholly'* or *'entirely'*]. May your *whole* spirit, soul and body be kept blameless at the coming of our Lord Jesus Christ.'

This is a magnificent but mysterious hope. How on earth is this going to happen? God will have do some major work on me to achieve this! The question has been intensifying all along: 1 Thessalonians 3:13 … 4:3 … Now the extraordinary prospect of entire sanctification is placed before us. How and when will this happen? In my lifetime? Will death somehow find me entirely sanctified? Or will some post-death purgatory complete the job? No!

No, this entire sanctification is not placed in my lifetime or when I die but when He comes again. It is not death that will perfect us but His *parousia*. Didn't we say that God would have to do an extraordinary work to achieve our entire sanctification? Well, says Paul – it is precisely and only God who can be trusted to do it – 'May God himself …'

And we are not surprised to learn that Paul invokes this God who, he aptly reminds us, is the 'God of peace'. 'Peace' has its deep biblical echoes of *shalom* – of integrity and harmony and the resolving of all dissonance and the bringing of what is fragmented together. The God of wholeness and completeness will sanctify us wholly.

It is this God of peace who will do what only God can do. Our salvation – in the sense the writer to Hebrews also employed later (Heb. 9:28) – is brought to completion at Christ's coming. Paul will later speak to the Corinthians of the day 'when perfection comes' (1 Cor. 13:10). This must be the answer to our question – how and when?

Meanwhile we must follow the instructions we are given, in 1 Thessalonians 5:12–22. It is very striking in verses 12–22 that Paul assumes that the community together will grow to care for itself with the 'one another' ministries he has highlighted before.

Dwell on just one focus of pastoral care for a moment – the people Paul identifies in verse 14 as the 'timid' (NIV) or 'fainthearted' (NRSV). These are literally the 'small-souled'. Here the focus is on the lack of what P.T. Forsyth called 'soul greatness'.[42] This is a condition where our capacity for faith and hope is diminished, has shrivelled or is underdeveloped. It is the result of feeding on trivialities and titbits. No soul will grow big in God if it seeks to exist on spiritual junk food.

To expand and grow the soul we will need to absorb the big themes and the objective truths of our faith. We will need to feed on the majestic facts of God's holiness and love, the incarnation of the Son of God and the victory of His cross and resurrection; we will need to embrace the soul-stretching vision of His *parousia*.

As Robert Barron puts it:

> Light in the darkness, the mocker of the grave, divine love in the most God-forsaken places, Jesus throws off balance the whole world of the *small soul.*
>
> Anxiety, depression, failure, sin, disease, death itself are no longer places where the *pusilla anima* can stake out its independence, establish its realm. They have all been invaded and conquered by Jesus, the one who raises the dead.[43]

To which might be added the need to embrace the soul-stretching vision Paul offers us here of the glorious, grace-filled coming again of our blessed Lord Jesus Christ. *In other words, what we need in order to recover soul-greatness is less therapy and more theology.*

Take seriously Paul's admonition in verse 19: 'Do not put out the Spirit's fire' (NIV); 'Do not quench the Spirit' (NRSV). Paul's emphasis here on peace, orderliness, discipline and holiness is not meant to curb our freedom but to facilitate it. We totally misunderstand Paul if we read him as advocating a 'play-it-safe' kind of Christianity. Paul would not recognise a church that hunkers down into a safe and cosy bunker, keeping its head beneath the parapet of risky living and sitting out this evil world until the second coming.

No, that's not his vision, not in a million years.

Paul wants expansive faith and abounding love and unrepressed joy and uninhibited praise. Paul expects in every church to see an overflowing of the fullness and flourishing of all the Spirit's powers and gifts. He is well aware, as we are, that there is no fire without smoke – and that sometimes irritatingly the smoke gets in our eyes. But his answer then and now would always be – never damp the Spirit's fire, never despise His gifts, however partially they come.

As Barry Callen wisely argues: 'In Christian discipleship, there is an important place for a kind of extravagance, a yielding to the excessive, a stepping out of the usual paths.' Too often, Callen observes, the Church inhabits a wonder-less world, which provokes no sense of amazement or interest in the watching public. But, he says, 'Vision and adoration should dominate our lives – and spill over to others.'[44]

Our incentive? The prospect of there being one day a full and satisfactory answer to Paul's prayer for us: 'May God himself, the God of peace, sanctify you through and through ['wholly' or 'entirely']. May your whole spirit, soul and body be kept blameless at the coming of our Lord Jesus Christ.'

- Meanwhile … we must respect and follow leadership in the Church (vv.12–13) because until perfection comes we will need to be taught, guided, supervised and cared for on the way; until He comes in all His glory, Who is our Master and Commander, who outranks us all and who will on that day render all offices and ministries redundant.
- We will need to encourage and admonish one another on the way (see vv.12–14) because until He comes the community of faith is unfinished and will have its weak spots, be fainthearted and workshy … and patience will be called for until perfection comes.
- We have to be commanded to rejoice (v.16) because our praise is incomplete and will remain so until that day when all creation

is freed from its frustration to sing the One Creator's song and all is lost in wonder, love and perfect praise.

- We have to be told not to quench the Spirit (v.19), because until the perfect comes we have an incurable tendency to lapse into the flesh, to institutionalise our freedoms, and to turn movements into monuments ... and only when He comes will the Spirit in us at last burn wholly clear and free of smoke.
- We have to be told not to despise prophesying (v.20) because until the perfect comes, we will need the gift of prophecy, however pitiful and pathetic it can sometimes be, to keep on nudging us in the Spirit in the direction of God's future.
- We have to test everything (v.21), holding fast to what is good, because until He comes all is mixed, every prophecy is partial and needs to be sifted, and every good thing so easily slips from our grasp. Until He comes there remains the need to exercise self-control in the face of provocation and to avoid even the semblance of evil.
- And meanwhile ... we have to pray unceasingly (v.17), as if our lives depended on it, because only when He comes will we know if He finds faith on the earth or in His Church.

So, all Paul's powers are geared to assuring the Thessalonians and us that the Day of the Lord is coming and, when it comes, will be the Day of Completion. When our complete Saviour returns he will come to complete our salvation. His *parousia* will bring our perfection with it.

One day the scaffolding that has obscured the Church – masking the reason for the noises and hammer blows, and mess and dust, and the need often for hard hats – that scaffolding will be taken down and we shall appear as we have been intended to be. The 'sons of God' will be revealed.

God will do it as only He can. 'The one who calls you is faithful and he will do it' (v.24).

James Denney writes:

> When we pray to God to sanctify us wholly ... is not our confidence this, that God has called us to this life of entire consecration, that He has opened the door for us enter upon it by sending His Son to be a propitiation for our sins, that He has actually begun it by inclining our hearts to receive the gospel, and that He may be depended upon to persevere in it till it is thoroughly accomplished?

Denney goes on to ask further:

> What would all our good resolutions amount to, if they were not backed by the unchanging purpose of God's love? What would be the worth of all our efforts and all of our hopes, if behind them, and behind our despondency and our failures too, there did not stand the unwearying faithfulness of God?
>
> This is the rock which is higher than we; our refuge; our stronghold; our stay in time of trouble. The gifts and calling of God are without repentance. We may change, but not He.[45]

5:25-28

[25]Brothers, pray for us. [26]Greet all the brothers with a holy kiss. [27]I charge you before the Lord to have this letter read to all the brothers [28]The grace of our Lord Jesus Christ be with you all.

Grace will win at last. Paul ends this letter as he will end all his subsequent letters, signing off on the note of grace.

John Piper notes that all Paul's letters begin and end with grace. But he helpfully draws our attention to an interesting variation. He points out that without exception the blessings *at the beginning* of the letters say, 'Grace *to* you ...' That is true here in

1 Thessalonians 1:1. But the blessings *at the end* always say, 'Grace be *with you*.' So it is here 5:28.

Piper then goes on to suggest that

> at the beginning of his letters Paul has in mind that the letter itself is a channel of God's grace *to* the readers. Grace is about to flow from God through Paul's writings *to* the Christians ... But as the end of the letter approaches, Paul realizes that reading is almost finished

– or in our case, is finished –

> and the question arises, 'What becomes of the grace that has been flowing through the reading of the inspired letter?' He answers with a blessing at the end of every letter: 'Grace (be) *with you*'. *With* you as you put the letter away and leave the church. *With* you as you go home to deal with a sick child and an unaffectionate spouse. *With* you as you go to work and face the temptations of anger and dishonesty and lust. *With* you as you muster courage to speak up for Christ over lunch.[46]

Grace never fails. All good things come to an end; but the one good thing that never comes to an end is God. It will all turn out right in the end, some say. Will it? It will for those who cast themselves wholly and entirely on this faithful God and His unfailing saving and sanctifying grace. It will for those who believe that the End God has in store for us in Christ will make it all right.

Meanwhile – 1 Thessalonians 5:25–27 – do the simple things and do them well.

- Greet one another with a holy kiss;
- Pray for one another;
- And be sure to read aloud this Spirit-inspired letter in the congregation over and over again until we get the glorious point, and feed ourselves on grace until He comes to complete the work He has begun in us.

Prayer and Reflection

Wholeness so often seems a distant dream, Lord.
Our lives are so fragmented ...
    ... distracted by divergent demands,
    ... torn apart by rival claims on our attention,
    ... compartmentalised by the various 'roles' we have to play,
    ... frustrated by so much left undone, started and left ...
unfinished ...

Lord,
Only You can gather up all the lost fragments.
Only You can piece together the precious shards of potential.
Only You can retrieve the lost good and redeem the lost love.

One day,

Sin, my worst enemy before,
Shall vex my eyes and ears no more,
My inward foes shall all be slain,
Nor Satan break my peace again.

Speed that day of perfection, Lord.

Meanwhile, 'unite my heart to fear Your name', focus my
distracted attention on the one thing needful, collect my scattered
energies into the one thing worth doing.
In Jesus' name,
Amen.

- Reflect on the wisdom needed on the one hand not to 'quench the Spirit' and, on the other, to 'test everything'.
- Compose your own prayer asking God to make you whole.

2 THESSALONIANS

1:1-5 Great news about the Church

1:1-2

¹Paul, Silas and Timothy,

To the church of the Thessalonians in God our Father and the Lord Jesus Christ:

²Grace and peace to you from God the Father and the Lord Jesus Christ.

In all likelihood it was a matter of months after writing his first letter to the church in Thessalonica that Paul wrote again. Three issues which he had touched on in the first letter surface again, and Paul's treatment of them provides a rough outline to his second letter.

1. There is continuing affliction and persecution, dealt with in 2 Thessalonians 1:1–10.
Prayer wish 1:11–12

2. There is misunderstanding about the second coming, dealt with in 2 Thessalonians 2:1–12.
Thanksgiving and prayer 2:13–3:5

3. There is a worsening problem with the 'unruly idle', dealt with in 2 Thessalonians 3:6–15.
Prayer wish 3:16–18

1:3-5

³We ought always to thank God for you, brothers, and rightly so, because your faith is growing more and more, and the love every one

of you has for each other is increasing. ⁴Therefore, among God's churches we boast about your perseverance and faith in all the persecutions and trials you are enduring.

⁵All this is evidence that God's judgment is right, and as a result you will be counted worthy of the kingdom of God, for which you are suffering.

Paul begins the letter with a characteristic burst of praise. In fact, verses 3–10 constitute one long sentence in the Greek text. This should be borne in mind as we face up to the tough things Paul says later in this section. Paul never speaks as a detached theologian. His theological thinking is being done 'on the job' and white-hot. It brims with passion and flares up with praise. Theology for Paul is always doxology.

Paul is thankful to God that his hopes for the Thessalonians have been richly realised. Their faith which he had thought might be defective is growing, and their love for one another – far from waning – is increasing (v.3; cf 1 Thess. 3:10,12). The 'model' church whose fame spread throughout the region (1 Thess. 1:7–8) now makes him even prouder because of the way it is enduring affliction (v.4).

As we noted in reflecting on the first letter, Paul regards 'affliction' – the social and perhaps physical consequences of conversion – as 'par for the course'. This is not simply because it is inevitable. Rather, suffering for Christ is transfigured by being taken up into God's larger scheme of things for establishing His kingdom. When viewed in the widest perspective, that of the ultimate and 'righteous judgment' of God, such suffering becomes a badge, if not of identity then certainly of honour – a mark of being worthy for the kingdom.

Willingness to suffer or even die for one's faith is not, of course, the final proof that it is true – as the current epidemic of suicide-bombers shows. There is surely a world of difference between the fanaticism that courts pain or inflicts suffering in order to pursue its goals, and the faith that is staunch enough to submit to unjust suffering because it trusts in the ultimate vindication of a righteous and just God. In this, the early Christians are, as we say, a hard act to follow. It is sometimes argued that the ancient world was ripe for the gospel, and there is some truth to this. But it scarcely accounts for the courage of all those who paid the cost to follow Christ. As Tom Wright says:

> Christianity summoned proud pagans to face torture and death out of loyalty to a Jewish villager who had been executed by Rome. Christianity advocated a love which cut across racial boundaries. It sternly forbade sexual immorality, the exposure of children, and a great many other things which the pagan world took for granted. Choosing to become a Christian was not an easy or natural thing for the average pagan.[1]

Hope for the coming kingdom was no doubt a key incentive in sustaining the believers when they came under pressure. But the prospect held before them was not some self-indulgent fantasy of bliss with 70 vestal virgins, but the God-centred ambition of being counted worthy of the kingdom and of sharing in the glory of the King (cf vv.10–11).

We have noted before the strong Jewish tradition, reflected in the New Testament (eg, Isa. 66:7–8; Rom. 8:22f.; Col. 1:24), which believes suffering may even count as part of the birth pangs of the coming Messianic age.[2]

For Christians then and in many parts of our world today – in the Sudan or Indonesia, Pakistan or Nigeria perhaps – Paul's words ring true as a fact of daily life. To quote one Christian from Malaku, recent massacres and expulsions in that region are 'according to God's plan. Christians are under purification from the Lord.' As a current Sudanese liturgy confesses, 'Death has come to reveal the faith; it has begun with us and it will end with us.'[3]

The pressure then as now is to invest all our trust in the empire of human beings to fulfil our dreams. But as Michael Gorman suggests, Paul

> urges his readers from Thessalonica to Corinth to Philippi and to Rome to accept an alternative hope, one grounded in love and cruciform power rather than violence, one offering true peace and security (cf 1 Thess. 5:3) through loyalty to God in Jesus rather than to the emperor. This, for Paul, is a certain hope, a confidence that the sufferings of this present age are mysteriously the firstfruits and guarantor of the true glory to come, not of Rome, but of God.[4]

1:6–10 Good news of God's justice

[6]God is just: He will pay back trouble to those who trouble you [7]and give relief to you who are troubled, and to us as well. This will happen when the Lord Jesus is revealed from heaven in blazing fire with his powerful angels. [8]He will punish those who do not know God and do not obey the gospel of our Lord Jesus. [9]They will be punished with everlasting destruction and shut out from the presence of the Lord and from the majesty of his power [10]on the day he comes to be glorified in his holy people and to be marvelled at among all those who have believed. This includes you, because you believed our testimony to you.

This piece of the text is at once fascinating and frightening. It poses the starkest of alternative destinies – retribution or rest, destructive punishment or dazzling glory. And all at the final revelation of Jesus Christ. The 'unveiling' of Jesus (His 'apocalypse'), in all His majestic glory, is pictured by Paul in traditional apocalyptic colours – 'blazing fire and angels' (v.7, cf Isa. 66:15–16; Psa. 68:17).

His coming exposes a decisive division between those 'who do not know God', including those who 'do not obey the gospel of our

Lord Jesus' (v.8 – terms often used to refer respectively to Gentiles and to Jews but here more likely to refer to both pagan and Jewish enemies of the Church) *and* those who are marked out as God's 'holy people' who believed the apostolic 'testimony' (v.10).

On the one hand are the afflicted for whom there is relief in being with the Lord for ever; on the other hand are the afflictors for whom there is only ruin and banishment from the Lord's presence and majesty (vv.7,9). For believers there is, above all, the stunning prospect of being immersed in the majestic glory of the Lord and marvelling at the unveiling of His matchless glory (v.10).

This is tough talk. What can we make of it? I offer several reflections.

1. We naturally demand justice

It was unwise of President Bush to style the response to the terrorist atrocities of 11 September 2001 'operation infinite justice'. We should not have needed our Muslim friends to point out that only God can dispense justice of this quality. And face *His* justice we must, terrorist and terrorised equally.

As I write, Britain's worst serial killer, Dr Harold Shipman, has just committed suicide only a year or two into a life sentence for the murder of dozens of his elderly patients and having been suspected of killing over 200 more. The tabloid press claimed to be speaking for the relatives of his victims in screaming headlines to the effect that 'he cheated justice'. Did he? Does any of us, in the end, cheat justice? The answer is 'no'.

But would it matter if we could? Surely here the answer is 'yes'. It is certainly rare to find anyone – except psychopaths, Shipman included – who does not have an innate sense of outrage when injustice is done and got away with. Most of us, even in our morally indifferent era, have a deep inner desire to see wrongs righted and the world made good.

Os Guinness as usual offers perceptive comment:

> Face to face with raw and naked evil, our relativism, non-judgmentalism, and even atheism count for nothing. Absolute evil calls for absolute judgment. Instinctively and intuitively, we cry out for the unconditional to condemn evil unconditionally.[5]

This is exactly the justice that is promised.

2. We fear justice and seek to avoid it!

The fact of judgment is a necessary message in every age, not least in our modern world of moral relativism. We want justice, but usually for others! There is a widespread refusal to accept responsibility for our actions.

* The vast majority of AIDS victims outside of Africa are practising homosexuals who clamour for a pill to cure the disease so that they may escape the consequences of their perversion and carry on with an immoral lifestyle.
* Those who think it's chic to dabble in recreational drugs deny they have opened the door to addiction and self-destructive criminality.
* What were the sharp office practices that eventually led to corporate business corruption on an Enron scale?

None of us is immune from the sinful refusal to be responsible for the outcome of our actions. In our victim-mentality culture we are only too eager to demand justice provided it is other people who are being blamed and castigated.

The Day of the Lord is a threat only to those who have 'refused to love the truth' as it confronts us in the gospel (2 Thess. 2:10b).

3.Christians should handle texts like this about judgment with sensitivity and care

Before we rush to judgment and consign most of our fellow human beings to the flames of eternal torment, we might pause to consider Paul's aim and methods in speaking in the way that he does. First, Paul is deliberately using the lurid language of apocalyptic, which paints in bold and primary colours. It sharply delineates good from evil and in this way forces us to face ultimate issues. But apocalyptic deals in pictorial imagery and the metaphor of poetry, and resists being forced into literalistic prose statements.[6]

It needs to be borne in mind also that the apocalyptic message is for special times and needs, 'given to those whose social and cultural worlds are collapsing'.[7]

Second, Paul is here speaking *to believers*. He speaks passionately and vividly to *persecuted* Christians to remind them of the rightness of their cause and their ultimate vindication by God, the Judge of all. Paul is *not directly* addressing the topic of the fate of the unbelieving in general. He is guaranteeing to the afflicted Christians in Thessalonica that those who are afflicting them will get their comeuppance and will surely pay for their violence. Evil, he reassures them, will not have the last word.

4.The justice of God is always and finally good news

Does qualifying the bald statements of Scripture about judgment, as I have done, mean that modern Christians have gone soft on sin and judgment? Well, perhaps. There are those in the Church who mourn the passing of 'fire and brimstone' preaching: 'Where is the hell we have known and loved?'! I do not share their sense of loss. If you cannot preach judgment as part of the gospel of grace then you had better not preach it at all.

With its Old Testament roots, the justice of God encompasses far more than punishment and goes well beyond retribution. In Scripture, God's justice is the righting of wrongs, the rectifying of injustices, the vindication of the victimised, the making whole and making good of all God's spoiled creation.

'The *Last Judgment*,' writes Robert Jenson,

> ... will be an act of God in which the accumulated injustice of history ... is put right. I do not mean to deny that individuals will indeed be judged ... And perhaps this will not be accomplished without excluding some from the blessed community altogether, so that indeed there comes to be a final community of love and another one of hatred, called hell. But the primary reality of what we may await is the establishing of universal and perfect justice, which on the biblical understanding of justice, is the same as the establishing of universal and perfect love.[8]

Our hearts ache for this – for compensation in another world of all that has been so painfully amiss in this one. If this, to any degree, is what the Day of the Lord entails, then it offers a glorious hope. Holding fast then to the legacy of the prophets and apostles, we celebrate the good news of God's justice.

We rest in two considerations:

- We know by revelation that there is no alternative to the gospel. Yet we know from experience that through this gospel this God loves His enemies and justifies the ungodly.
- It is enough to know that 'God is just' (v.6); in this God we trust!

1:11–12 Prayer report

> [11]With this in mind, we constantly pray for you, that our God may count you worthy of his calling, and that by his power he may fulfil every good purpose of yours and every act prompted by your faith.

[12]We pray this so that the name of our Lord Jesus may be glorified in you, and you in him, according to the grace of our God and the Lord Jesus Christ.

In the light of the solemn teaching and serious issues of the earlier part of this chapter, why not sink to your knees right now, take this prayer of Paul for the Thessalonians, and pray it for yourself?

Time seems to slip through our fingers. Our best intentions to serve God seem fragile and short-lived. What we do for the Lord doesn't seem to add up to much. We wonder if we have any lasting legacy.

The psalmist, keenly aware of the transience of life, confesses that 'our days ... quickly pass, and we fly away' (Psa. 90:10) and hastily pleads the favour of God, asking God to 'establish the work of our hands' (v.17).

In similar fashion Paul prays that God's power 'will effect in you all his goodness desires to do' (2 Thess. 1:11, Phillips). Early in his *Rule*, St Benedict counsels: 'Every time you begin a good work, you must pray to God most earnestly to bring it to perfection.'

The process which culminates in Jesus being glorified in his people (v.10) begins now (v.12) as grace takes the 'five loaves and two small fishes' of our faith in action and multiplies them to feed a crowd. He stakes His name on being able to make our little go a long way, and by doing with it far more than we can ask or even imagine.

And every virtue we possess,
and every victory won,
and every thought of holiness
are his alone.
> Harriet Auber

Prayer and Reflection

Lord, dare we celebrate the good news of Your justice?
The alternative is too awful to contemplate.
If falling into Your holy hands is in any way a fearful thing, it is infinitely better than falling out of them ...
... better, when all polls close, that Yours is the casting vote,
... better when all verdicts our passed, that Your judgment is the last court of appeal.
... better, when all is gathered in, that grace is Your final word.

The better world our hearts cry out for is
not ours to demand but Yours to give
not ours to deserve but Yours to bestow
Let your kingdom come, O Lord.

Meanwhile ...
... may faith keep growing,
... may love keep increasing,
... establish the work of our hands.
So speed the day when, in us or by us, Your majesty is marvelled at by all who are even now amazed by grace.

- Consider the horror of being denied justice and pray for known victims of injustice.
- What might we do to help fulfil the challenge of the prophet Amos, 'Let justice roll on like a river, righteousness like a never-failing stream'?

2:1–12 How evil works

2:1–2

[1]Concerning the coming of our Lord Jesus Christ and our being gathered to him, we ask you, brothers, [2]not to become easily unsettled or alarmed by some prophecy, report or letter supposed to have come from us, saying that the day of the Lord has already come.

These verses bring us to the heart of Paul's pastoral concern for the Thessalonians and show us the real reason why he wrote this second letter to them. The believers in Thessalonica are apparently being 'unsettled' and 'alarmed' by false teaching about the second coming of Christ. Paul aims to reassure them. He urges them to stand firm by holding fast to the teaching – particularly about eschatological matters – that he had originally given them and had reinforced in his first letter (cf 2 Thess 2:15).

So Paul writes to remind them of what he had taught them about the Lord's coming and our being gathered together to Him. In passing, it is worth noting that the Lord's coming (His *parousia*) and our being gathered together to Him (the so-called 'rapture' of 1 Thess. 4:17) are grammatically viewed in 2 Thessalonians 2:1 as *one event*. Some popular prophecy teachers today separate these two events when they say that the 'gathering together to Him' is a secret event that precedes the coming of the Lord. But there is absolutely no exegetical justification whatsoever for splitting them apart in that way.

More to the point is to notice how determined Paul is to counteract false teaching about the Lord's return that is disturbing the church at Thessalonica. Evidently there has been a serious distortion – perhaps a deliberate misrepresentation of Paul's original teaching – on the prospects for the future.

In particular he wants to quash the notion that 'the Day of the Lord has already come'. Just how the Thessalonians had come to entertain such an idea, whether 'through prophecy, word or letter' is unclear.

The text is rather odd and raises several questions. After all, if the 'Day of the Lord' signifies the end of our space–time world, it is difficult to conceive how anyone might imagine it had already happened or, stranger still, be informed of it by letter! Even if the concept of the Day of the Lord is stretched to make such a deduction possible, it is still hard to see how Paul might be held to be responsible for this.

It could scarcely have come through a prophecy or spiritual utterance Paul had given when he was with them, since it conflicts with his own teaching. Nor could he have given it subsequently, since he had not returned in person to Thessalonica. Nor did this occur by the spoken 'word', since Paul is very clear about what he did and did not teach when he founded the church. As for a 'letter', what can it refer to other than First Thessalonians or – as some scholars speculate – a forged letter purporting to be from Paul of which we have no record?

It is all rather strange, though there can be no doubt that Paul felt that his teaching had been seriously distorted and that the issue need to be firmly addressed.

Matters are clarified for us considerably, I believe, if closer attention is paid to the grammar of Paul's sentence. The contentious phrase is, literally, 'as though through us' (v.2), which is translated – in fact, paraphrased – somewhat tenuously by the NIV as 'supposed to have come from us'. This begs the question.

Gordon Fee has argued, convincingly to my mind, that the phrase 'as though through us' should be attached *not* to what *precedes it* but to the clause that *follows it*[9] – literally, 'nor by Spirit, nor by a word, nor by letter' – As Fee argues:

> Paul almost certainly does not mean, '*through* a letter, as though *from* us'; he means 'whether through (any of these means), as though through us the present teaching came to you'.[10]

In other words, Paul contends, there is no way in which the erroneous idea that says that the Day of the Lord has come can be attributed to him, no matter how it had arisen. Paul is concerned not so much about the *means* by which the teaching had come to the Thessalonians as about its *content*. He emphatically denies that his teaching could ever be misconstrued to the effect that one was able to conclude that the Day of the Lord had come.

If we still want to ask *how* this may have occurred, it may be helpful to compare 2 Thessalonians 2:2 with 2:15. In verse 2 Paul mentions a trio of possible agents – 'Spirit' (or 'prophecy' in the NIV), 'word, letter'. But he concludes his appeal by urging the Thessalonian Christians to stand firm in the apostolic tradition he has already established among them, 'whether by word of mouth or by letter' (v.15).

The omission of any reference to '*dia pneumatos*' ('by' or 'through the Spirit' – NIV: 'by some prophecy') may well be significant. It suggests that the false teaching had come into the church through a prophetic utterance assumed to have been inspired by the Holy Spirit.

Now Paul's answer to the abuse of the charismatic gifts is never disuse but right use. This resonates with 1 Thessalonians 5:19–21: 'Do not put out the Spirit's fire; do not treat prophecies with contempt. Test everything. Hold on to the good.'

Evaluation is crucial. Paul is everywhere keen to encourage spiritual utterances. At the same time he consistently insists on their being tested against the gold standard of the apostolic preaching and teaching of the gospel. Whatever disconnects with that must be rejected. Whatever agrees with the apostolic traditions is to be received as an endorsement of them.

To 'hold on to the good' (1 Thess. 5:21) means to stand firm by holding 'to the teachings we passed on to you' (2 Thess. 2:15).

Paul is writing this letter as a pastor. He wants the Thessalonians to 'keep [their] heads and not be thrown off … balance' (v.2, Phillips). He can immediately set their minds straight and put their hearts at rest. Before the Day of the Lord arrives, he reminds them, other significant and highly visible events must take place *first*; namely, the great 'rebellion' and the rise of the 'man of lawlessness' (v.3).

2:3-8

³Don't let anyone deceive you in any way, for that day will not come until the rebellion occurs and the man of lawlessness is revealed, the man doomed to destruction. ⁴He will oppose and will exalt himself over everything that is called God or is worshipped, so that he sets himself up in God's temple, proclaiming himself to be God.

⁵Don't you remember that when I was with you I used to tell you these things? ⁶And now you know what is holding him back, so that he may be revealed at the proper time. ⁷For the secret power of lawlessness is already at work; but the one who now holds it back will continue to do so till he is taken out of the way. ⁸And then the lawless one will be revealed, whom the Lord Jesus will overthrow with the breath of his mouth and destroy by the splendour of his coming.

This passage reminds me of what Winston Churchill said of Soviet Russia just prior to World War Two, when he described it as 'a riddle wrapped in a mystery inside an enigma'. The text ranks among the most difficult of all Paul's writings to decipher and, for that reason, has become a happy hunting ground for speculators. Better therefore to start with the big picture.

Lawlessness is terrifying. Anyone living under a totalitarian regime can bear witness to the horror and fear that lawlessness induces. A hammering on the door in the dead of night. Brusque commands and rough hands. Arbitrary arrests and imprisonment. No questions asked, no explanations given. No appeal, no one to speak for up you, no vindication, no justice.

The influential rich or politically powerful rise cynically 'above the law' or enact laws that serve their advantage. Perjury and false witnesses or, even worse, state-sponsored contract-killings occur. A lawless society is spawned in hell.

Michael Burleigh wisely exposes the roots of an ideology that gave us Auschwitz:

> One aspect of dictatorship seems in need of more emphasis than it nowadays tends to receive – the supercession of the rule of law by arbitrary police terror. This was not some prosaic B-movie before the A-movie of the regime's racial rampage, but the crucial break with the most fundamental characteristic of free societies.[11]

Nor is revolutionary upheaval all it's cracked up to be! Romantics are initially enticed by the heady revolutionary talk and ferment for change. But before long, the grey ideologues have taken over the people's uprising and then everything is bent to serve the idolatrous cause of 'the Revolution'. For the good of 'the Revolution', human rights are trampled on, civil liberties are curtailed, personal freedoms and dignities cynically and brutally overridden. Unspeakable injustice reigns. And all such scenarios, horribly familiar to anyone who reflects on the history of the twentieth century, are mere trailers for the big event to come.

So the 'rebellion' (v.3) that erupts in the apocalyptic scenario Paul paints opens the way for the 'man of lawlessness' to emerge. He is depicted (v.4) as the consummation of a godless humanism. God-defying and self-exalting, he is the ultimate 'Anarchist' (*The Message*). This figure both opposes God and seeks to supplant God, 'proclaiming himself to be God' (v.4).

The vivid description conjures up the ghosts of nightmare episodes in Jewish history as told in its own apocalyptic stories. Two centuries before Jesus, after the fourfold break up of Alexander the Great's massive Hellenistic Empire, the Seleucid warlord, Antiochus Epiphanes – the 'little horn' of Daniel 7 – crushed God's people and arrogantly despoiled the holiness of the Temple

(Dan. 7:25; 8:11; 11:31,36). In later periods of oppression, the Roman General Pompey, and the Emperor Caligula both desecrated the Temple in Jerusalem and set up idolatrous images in the holy place.

What are we to make of Paul's cryptic but powerful language? From our distance, much is uncertain, but the 'man of lawlessness' seems to be the culmination of all arrogant evil and self-exaltation, the manifestation of a mysterious underlying principle already and always at work among the fallen children of Adam (v.7).

Meanwhile there is some*thing* that 'holds him back' or 'restrains' (v.6) and some*one* who does the restraining (v.7). But Paul does not make clear the identity of the 'what' or 'who' that restrains. The Thessalonians knew to what or whom Paul was referring to ('you know ...' v.6) but we do not.

Much ink has been spilled in speculating about the identity of the 'restrainer'. The Roman Empire itself, in so far as it kept order, has been suggested as the 'restraining influence', with the emperor cast as the 'restrainer'. Others have placed the gospel or the Holy Spirit in this role, though it is impossible to see in what sense these are to be removed, except in some unbiblical, dispensationalist scheme of things.

Perhaps greater consideration might be given than has been given so far to the suggestion that the 'restraining influence' is *malignant, not benign*. In this case we might translate '*to katechon*' as the 'seizing power' (as Karl Donfried does following C.H. Giblin).[12] Even more helpful is to translate it as 'that which prevails' or 'holds sway', which Charles Wanamaker prefers.[13] This at least has the merit of introducing some symmetry to the passage. Looking at these verses in this way, and seeking a more literal approach to the Greek which Paul wrote, we might detect a *threefold* movement in the text.

The movement in all three cases is from speaking of a thing or force (ie speaking in *impersonal* terms using the neuter participle) which is largely a present reality, to speaking in *more personal* terms of one who is still future (using the masculine participle):

So the 'rebellion' (v.3a) ...

... comes to full expression in the revelation of the archetypal 'man of lawlessness' (v.3b)

So that which 'seizes' or 'prevails' (v.6a, *to katechon*, 'the prevailing power'?) is a force felt in the present ('you know ...')

... So that he (perhaps anticipating v.7 and *ho katechōn*, 'the prevailing one?') may be 'revealed in his own time' or 'when his time comes' (v.6b)

So the 'mystery of lawlessness' (v.7a), that 'Satanic counterpart of God's purpose' (F.F. Bruce) is already at work ...

... until 'the prevailing one' *ho katechōn* (perhaps Satan or the Roman emperor who is a front for Satanic power, as implied in 1 Cor. 2:6,8) 'comes from' or 'is gone from' the 'midst' (v.7b).[14]

This approach makes sense to me. All three statements are then about negative forces. It fits the context where Paul is probing the ramifications of evil; it offers an obvious parallelism; it keys in to the movement from an impersonal force to a personal embodiment of evil. Having said that, it remains unproven and unprovable among a range of options.

When all is said and done and all angles explored, we may do best to concede – with Augustine – that we do not, and cannot, know exactly what Paul and the Thessalonians had in mind in speaking in these terms. In the end, whether 'that which prevails' or 'restrains' plays a negative or positive part in the 'lawless one's' emergence, one thing is sure: his destruction is built-in, guaranteed. The lawless one is a 'son of destruction'; he is 'doomed to destruction' (v.3c).

Paul is so confident in the triumph of God in Christ over all evil powers that no sooner is the 'lawless one' spoken of as being revealed than he is written off as being utterly routed (v.8)! The spectre of this 'man of lawlessness' then undoubtedly looms large in Paul's apocalyptic vision. But who exactly he is, or might be, Paul does not make clear.

This reticence on Paul's part is perennially resented by many sensation-starved and curious Christians who have proceeded confidently to fill in the blanks with the names of suitable candidates from the medieval Popes, through Napoleon and Hitler down to Henry Kissinger and Bill Gates. All this would be risible were it not for the fact that it devours so much energy and money and attracts such obsessive interest among fundamentalist and evangelical Christians.

It's no doubt a vain hope, but one cannot help longing for the day when a certain section of evangelicalism might outgrow its adolescent fantasies and be happy to see its Christian 'science-fiction' and pop-prophecy well and truly left behind.

More serious is the way such so-called prophetic teaching – albeit unwittingly – detracts from the main thrust and joy of Paul's message – which is the total and absolute triumph of Christ over all God's enemies. If we can be sure of nothing else, we can be sure of this: the 'Day of the Lord' will be the Lord's day and His alone!

This is the tale of two rival comings. The 'lawless one' will have his *parousia* (v.9) but will be annihilated at the *parousia* of the Lord Jesus (v.8). Righteousness routs lawlessness. Reconciliation trumps rebellion. In that Day, nothing will prevail but sovereign love, and no one will hold sway but the Christ of God.

2:9-12

> ⁹The coming of the lawless one will be in accordance with the work of Satan displayed in all kinds of counterfeit miracles, signs and wonders, ¹⁰and in every sort of evil that deceives those who are perishing. They perish because they refused to love the truth and so be saved. ¹¹For this reason God sends them a powerful delusion so that they will believe the lie ¹²and so that all will be condemned who have not believed the truth but have delighted in wickedness.

Once more we face tough talk. What the final day will brutally expose is now made clear for the warning and wisdom of the saints of God; namely, the virulence and cunning of satanic power. The *parousia* of the 'lawless one' will bring to a fitting climax the long history of satanically inspired supernatural signs and satanically motivated acts of evil.

These miracles – we shudder to acknowledge – are not counterfeit in the sense of being unreal and only looking like miracles. No, these are actual miracles but ones that are sourced by an unholy spirit, bent on deception. They do not deceive the faithful, of course, but they serve to *harden* the unbelief of those already committed to the path of untruth. It is in this sense that we must take the strong causal phrase, 'God sends them a powerful delusion' (v.11). Just as He once did with Pharaoh, God will do with all who have already so indulged themselves in lies and pledged themselves to falsehood that they end up relishing wickedness (v.12).

The Caesars and Herods of this world will always crucify the Christ because when the Truth Himself stands before them they cannot see it, so inured are they in a lying and deceptive world-view (see again 1 Cor. 2:6–9). If we throw in our lot with 'antichrists' like these, we deceive ourselves and doom ourselves to go down with them to destruction.

Ideas do have consequences. Despite all postmodern nit-picking, truth is absolute and truth is crucial. And truth is not a set of propositions but the gospel itself. To reject God's offer of truth is a fatal move away from reality. To embrace the gospel with faith means rescue for the perishing.

2:13-15 How God works

2:13-14

> [13]But we ought always to thank God for you, brothers loved by the Lord, because from the beginning God chose you to be saved through the sanctifying work of the Spirit and through belief in the truth. [14]He called you to this through our gospel, that you might share in the glory of our Lord Jesus Christ.

To believe the truth is to love the truth; no more so than when God's truth comes home to the heart in such sweeping and stunning terms as this. What an extraordinary contrast to what has just been described.

- How evil works in the world (vv.3–12)
- How God works in the world (vv.13–14)

'The first half of this chapter,' says James Denney, 'is mysterious, awful and oppressive.' But 'another prospect looms larger for Paul and he fixes his eyes upon it, serene, bright and joyful.'[15]

Evil wreaks havoc in the world, working its unholy magic with an inherent, self-destructive violence to which it is totally blind. It spawns rebellion and breeds ruination for all its offspring. Evil embodies itself in the lawless in every age, and personifies itself in the ultimate man of lawlessness.

By contrast, God works to heal and rescue, to mend and reclaim. Love rules His every move. Where evil takes human shape in a man of lawlessness, God is incarnated in the truly human One, Jesus, the Son of Righteousness, Who is faithful and true. He works through His own Holy Spirit confounding the deception of satanic powers to rescue those He loves through faith in the truth of the gospel. The destiny to which He moves them is not ruin and destruction but salvation and glory. At every turn, God's sweet, fresh, bracing air of truth blows away the fog of lies and propaganda.

Everything about our salvation, whether past, present or future, has God's hallmark on it. The *source, means, implementation* and *end* of our salvation are all His work and design!

The *source* of our salvation is His election and love; its *origin* is in His initiative (v.13a). What sweeter music can we hear than to be told we are 'loved by the Lord' (v.13)? At this point, Paul is referring to the love of the Lord Jesus in whom the love of the Father (v.16) has been incarnated and which has captured our hearts.

'The people God loves' is all that is needed to describe us. Such love, fleshed out in Jesus and founded in the gospel of the cross, is enough to convince us that God's choice matters more to us than our own. Believers live in the freedom of lives that are not self-generated but God-given.

At this point it is useful to note a variation in the Greek text of the letter over which a decision has to be made by translators. Some manuscripts read here the word *aparchen* – which means 'firstfruits' (as in Rom. 8:23; James 1:18). Others equally authoritative read the word as *aparches* – which means 'beginning'. This latter word fits well the context and later Pauline theology and so most commentaries and translations, including the NIV, opt for 'God chose us *from the beginning*'.

However, this is unlikely to be the case. Gordon Fee points out that the normal rule of textual analysis argues that the harder reading must be preferred. That is, it is more likely that a scribe in copying the text might read *aparchen* and accidentally alter it to *aparches* (beginning). But there seems no conceivable exegetical or theological reason why he would do so the other way around. Therefore, *aparchen* is to be preferred as the original reading.

'God chose us' for salvation – as he chose Israel before – not to be a self-righteous ghetto of the saved but for the sake of sinners. The Thessalonian believers, small in number as they may be at present, are being encouraged by Paul to believe that they are but the 'firstfruits' of a much larger harvest in Thessalonica to be brought in by the gospel. The Thessalonian believers were the firstfruits of God's dream

> At a time of imperial expansion, economic injustice, and rising social tensions, Paul was beginning to forge an empire-wide movement of suffering and disenfranchised people who dreamed of being the beneficiaries, not the victims, of an all-powerful emperor.[16]

The *means* of salvation are the means God provides, which have to do specifically with the love shown us by our Lord Jesus Christ (v.16) and with the Spirit's sanctifying activity (v.13c). 'God chose you to be saved through the sanctifying work of the Spirit ...'

For any readers of this book who are steeped in evangelical piety, this is an unusual way of referring to 'sanctification' (*hagiasmos*). Usually 'sanctification' is applied to the *ongoing* process of holiness in our lives (cf 1 Thess. 4:3). But here it is being used in a way closer to its original connotation of 'consecration to' or being 'set apart for' God. The letter to the Hebrews talks of sanctification in a similar way, to refer to the radical change wrought by conversion (cf Heb. 2:11; 10:10; and cf

Heb. 9:14 with 1 Thess. 1:10).

Contrary to much accepted wisdom, Paul never did split justification and sanctification in the way later evangelical theology did. For him 'sanctification' applies to conversion. It highlights just that radical turning from previous allegiances to belong to and serve the living God that he had noted in 1 Thessalonians 1:10.

Paul was not averse to using the terminology of 'sanctification' as another metaphor alongside 'justification' – and others – to describe what happens in salvation (eg 1 Cor. 6:11).

To be set apart in this way for God and for God's holiness is appropriately the distinctive role the Holy Spirit plays in the trauma of conversion. Having started in this way, we are enlisted into a lifetime's progressive holiness in which we are guided, taught and empowered by the same Holy Spirit.

The *implementation* of our salvation is also God's work; He calls us through the gospel to believe in the truth. This too is a remarkable statement and one which contemporary evangelicalism would do well to take to heart. The gospel has the power to create a hearing for itself among an otherwise inattentive audience. When the gospel is proclaimed it carries with it the ability to evoke faith in unbelieving hearts. The gospel penetrates mental and spiritual defences. Its inherent persuasiveness woos and wins our hearts and lays claim to our obedient response. In the gospel the voice of the living God sounds forth to rouse the deaf and raise the dead.

The *end* for which we are saved is God's design and purpose. God's call issued through the message of the gospel is the stunning invitation to share in the glory that Jesus enjoys at the right hand of God.

Some Christians become nervous with the words, 'God chose you.' They fear an alien power that is arbitrary and selective on a whim. But if we are to be biblical at all we need to embrace these words with joy and confidence. In our modern world, choice is a matter of preference among a range of consumer options; and election is a mere political event. But in the Bible, election is the language of love and relationship (cf Deut. 7:7ff.). God set his love upon Israel. So God chooses to love.' He does not love us reluctantly or grudgingly or against His better judgment. God is gracious in taking initiatives in our lives. God moves towards us before we ever move towards Him. God acts to save us, God calls us, God keeps us to share His glory. No wonder Paul feels under obligation to give thanks to God for being such a God!

We might do well to pause and relish this magnificent statement. Here is truth about us and our future that is 'truth to be loved' as well as relied upon. Read verses 13–14 again right now and rejoice in this truth once again.

What James Denney said of this section (2 Thess. 2:13–14) of the Thessalonian letters might well be applied to all of them:

> One cannot read these … verses without wondering at the new world which the gospel created for the mind of man. What great thoughts are in them – thoughts that wander through eternity, thoughts based on the most sure and blessed of experiences, yet travelling back into the infinite past, and on into immortal glory; thoughts of the Divine presence and the Divine power interpenetrating and redeeming human life; thoughts addressed originally to a little company of working people but unmatched for length and breadth and height by all that pagan literature could offer to the wisest and the best.[17]

2:15

[15]So then, brothers, stand firm and hold to the teachings we passed on to you, whether by word of mouth or by letter.

For moderns the very idea – expressed in verse 15 – that we may be dependent on the testimony of others – especially of those long dead – is an affront to our autonomy and self-esteem. We prefer to make it up as we go along, disdainful of the accumulated wisdom of the past, suspicious of inherited ideas, disparaging even about the old among us.

There is of course much that needs to be jettisoned. But we disenfranchise ourselves if we cut ourselves off from our own history of grace. It is useful to be reminded of the oft-quoted distinction made by leading church historian, Jaroslav Pelikan, when he said that 'tradition is the living faith of the dead; traditionalism is the dead faith of the living'.[18] Of the apostles, above all, it can truly be said: 'Being dead they speak.'

So here, in verse 15, in speaking of the teachings 'we passed on to you', Paul is employing the technical terminology for the transmission of truth as received tradition (*paradosis*; cf. 1 Cor. 11:23).

What is worth noting is that here it refers to the deposit of apostolic teaching and practice with the apostolic gospel at its core, which is meant to be the touchstone of truth in the Church. This tradition is the 'faith that was once for all entrusted to the saints' (Jude 3), which later became the key criterion for assessing which inspired writings of the early Church should be recognised as part of the canon of Scripture. The apostolic teaching and gospel constitute the title-deeds of our faith, which we are not at liberty to change. To hold firmly to them is to remain part of the 'one holy, catholic and apostolic Church'.

Paradoxical though it may seem; we can choose to be self-made people, which is no choice at all; or we can choose to be chosen people, which is perfect freedom! We can live lives that are utterly self determined. In which case, as we do our own sinning, we must do our own saving. Or we can accept the God-bestowed and God-directed life, relishing the love that chooses us and saves us and calls us to share its glory. Who would ever want to move away from that?

2:16–17 Prayer wish

[16]May our Lord Jesus Christ himself and God our Father, who loved us and by his grace gave us eternal encouragement and good hope, [17]encourage your hearts and strengthen you in every good deed and word.

Those who through faith in the truth of the gospel are sanctified by the Holy Spirit have been enfolded in the love of God the Father and the Lord Jesus Christ. The Christian view of God is implicitly Trinitarian from its earliest days.

Where would all our good intentions come to if they were not capable of being carried through to successful outcome by the grace of God invested in us? Fragile hearts are made bravehearts in the courage God supplies; our weak resolve is strengthened by the hope set before us. By His grace, our best intentions are made good; our good deeds are made better; our best words are made flesh.

O little heart of mine! Shall pain
Or sorrow make thee moan?
When *all this God is all for thee,*
A Father all thine own?[19]

Prayer and Reflection

Lord, the workings of evil in the world baffle us.

We look into our own hearts and still see the attraction of rebellion and lawlessness.

We feel the pull of the undertow of sin that corrupts the good and aborts the best.

Forgive us for flirting with sin, and fondling its memories.

Lord, the workings of Your grace astonish us.

Thank You that evil's worst is no match for Your best.

We celebrate the mystery of Your activity:

of Your grace that is more original than sin;

of Your love that is the very soil in which we take root;

of Your choice that makes and keeps us free;

of Your salvation in Jesus Christ that makes us firstfruits

of your human harvest.

Thank You that when all is said and done, what counts is what You have said and done.

Thank You for the gospel.

Stir us to love the truth as well as believe it.

Encourage us in good hope.

Empower us for good deeds.

In Jesus' name,

Amen.

- Watch a TV soap opera alongside the news and note the signs of rebelliousness, lawlessness and the spurious glamour of godless living. Pray for revival.
- Read 2 Thessalonians 2:13–15 over again. Dwell on the reality of God's working in the world and in your life, and then turn your reflections into praise and worship.

3:1-5 **Prayer request**

¹Finally, brothers, pray for us that the message of the Lord may spread rapidly and be honoured, just as it was with you. ²And pray that we may be delivered from wicked and evil men, for not everyone has faith. ³But the Lord is faithful, and he will strengthen and protect you from the evil one. ⁴We have confidence in the Lord that you are doing and will continue to do the things we command. ⁵May the Lord direct your hearts into God's love and Christ's perseverance.

Paul's prayer request to the Thessalonians is followed by his prayer for them. Prayer is offered for:

- progress of the message;
- protection of the messengers;
- perseverance of the saints.

Paul asks the Thessalonians to pray for two things: first, 'that the message of the Lord may spread … and be honoured' (v.1). As always, Paul's overriding concern is for the rapid progress of the gospel and he urges the Thessalonians to pray to that end.

His words are vivid. Pray, he says, that the 'word of the Lord' may 'run …' Whether derived from the athletics for which Greece was famous or from echoes of Psalm 147:15 ('His word runs swiftly'), the words catch the urgency and passion of Paul's apostolic mission. Peterson captures it well: 'Pray that the Master's Word will simply take off and race through the country to a groundswell of response' (*The Message*).

The word of the Lord is 'glorified' when it is accepted and embraced as the truth so that God gets glory for the good news of salvation. 'The single most striking thing about early Christianity is its speed of growth.'[20] Within 30 years of the crucifixion, churches have been planted all around the Mediterranean world, even in Rome, the very heart of the Empire. We often overestimate the *size* of the churches in the first century – most of which were small enough to fit into an admittedly spacious house. But we should never underestimate this rapid expansion.

The believers in Thessalonica were indeed the 'firstfruits' (2 Thess. 2:13, NRSV) of a vast harvest, which is still being reaped today. Writing from where I am amid the noble ruins of European Christendom, it is easy to forget that Christianity is currently the fastest-growing faith on earth. Any readers of my words in Asia or Africa or Latin America will bear this out. If present growth rates continue, by 2050 there will be nearly as many *Pentecostal* Christians in the world as there are Moslems today! Christianity is truly a global phenomenon.[21]

But now as then, prayer is instrumental in this rapid spread of the gospel. The interaction between preaching and praying, between mission and intercession, is as mysterious as the sovereignty of God, Whose Spirit blows where He wills. But the effects are evident. And this is one reason why the invasion of human hearts by the gospel brings glory to God.

As John Piper puts it:

> Prayer is the walkie-talkie of the church on the battlefield of the world in the service of the word. It is not a domestic intercom to increase the comfort of the saints … It is for those on active duty. And in their hands it proves the supremacy of God in the pursuit of the nations. When mission moves forward by prayer it magnifies the power of God. When it moves by human management it magnifies man.[22]

How wonderful that the apostle Paul, the greatest church-planter of all, was not above needing or seeking the prayers of the churches he had established, so that the gospel might to be sent winging on its saving way.

Paul asks the Thessalonians to pray 'that we may be delivered from wicked and evil men' (v.2). The advance of the gospel does not go unopposed. Wherever the revolutionary message of the Lordship of Jesus spread, it threatened to turn the settled world upside down – just as it had done in Thessalonica (Acts 17:6). So the wicked and powerful have a vested interest in blocking the gospel's advance. As with Herod and Pilate in their unlikely conspiracy at the crucifixion, so evil men of power are a mere front for the evil one himself (cf 2 Thess. 3:3c; 1 Thess. 2:18). Paul himself already had the scars to show for the opposition the gospel aroused.

Despite this Paul is undaunted and remains confident that the Thessalonians too will stay the course (2 Thess. 3:3–4). He derives his confidence from the Lord (here again referring to the *Lord* Jesus) and especially from the Lord's faithfulness. The contrast with the opponents of the gospel is sharp, as we can see if we let verses 2 and 3 run together. Literally the text reads without a break: 'for not everyone has faith (*pistis*); faithful (*pistos*) however is the Lord ...'

The worst that evil can do is always met and matched by the best the Lord can do. Paul is sure that nothing will interfere with the Thessalonians' own growth and progress (v.4).

Paul's final prayer wish is not for himself but for them (v.5). Wavering hearts, disturbed by opposition, need to take shelter in the unyielding love God has for His people. Weak wills, shaken by hostile pressure, need to be tempered like steel in the determined courage shown by Jesus Christ Himself in face of every threat.

God's love endures for ever. Christ is committed to seeing through to the end what grace has started in our lives. He can no more fail in this than He can go back on His cross. As the old adage goes, the 'perseverance of the saints' is the perseverance of Christ *with* the saints. He is committed to you and me. He will not let us go or let us down. In Him is rock-solid reality.

3:6–12 Unruly idleness

⁶In the name of the Lord Jesus Christ, we command you, brothers, to keep away from every brother who is idle and does not live according to the teaching you received from us. ⁷For you yourselves know how you ought to follow our example. We were not idle when we were with you, ⁸nor did we eat anyone's food without paying for it. On the contrary, we worked night and day, labouring and toiling so that we would not be a burden to any of you. ⁹We did this, not because we do not have the right to such help, but in order to make ourselves a model for you to follow. ¹⁰For even when we were with you, we gave you this rule: 'If a man will not work, he shall not eat.'

¹¹We hear that some among you are idle. They are not busy; they are busybodies. ¹²Such people we command and urge in the Lord Jesus Christ to settle down and earn the bread they eat.

The crux of understanding this passage is: Who exactly are those whom Paul identifies as the 'idle' (vv.6,11)? The word *ataktoi* has the connotation of someone who has stepped 'out of line', and was used of pupils at school not lining up properly. As I can recall from experience, small boys in particular are never merely 'doing nothing' but are always liable to be 'up to mischief'!

The word *ataktoi* is therefore best translated as '*unruly* idle'. Indiscipline, not mere idleness, seems at the heart of the problem Paul is addressing. As he goes on to say of the 'idle', 'they are not busy; they are busybodies' (v.11b). In short, they are not simply being passively lazy but actively disruptive.

It is possible, as some commentators suggest, that the *ataktoi* are those Christians in Thessalonica who are so gripped with the imminence of Christ's return that they have given up work to wait for Him! This is an easy and rather obvious answer to our question.

Christian history is undoubtedly littered with examples of millenarian sects that have done just that. But this is an unlikely explanation for the issue that Paul is facing. He makes clear that the issue was not a consequence of his teaching on the second coming, or any distortion of it. In fact the problem was there from the beginning, when he was with them (v.10).

Misuse of the text

At this point it may be useful to dispose of two ways in which this passage is horribly misapplied.

- First, Paul's dictum in verse 10 – 'If a man will not work, he shall not eat' – is sometimes used as a stick with which to beat the unemployed. This is a total distortion of Paul's aim here. Paul's words are directed at those who have *deliberately chosen not to work* – 'if a man *will not* work' – not at those who are without work and through no fault of their own cannot get into the job market.
- Second, this text should never be used to oppose Government welfare schemes that help the vulnerable and needy in our society. This too would be a gross misrepresentation of Paul's teaching and intentions.

Can we come to a better understanding of Paul's exhortation here? Probing the first-century context may prove a better way into the text. This approach has led to the suggestion that the issue may have more to do with *social* conditions in Thessalonica than with eschatological fervour in the church.

Bruce Winter in particular has made a strong case for this view of what is going on.[23] He argues, persuasively to my mind, that the problem was caused by the social conventions of patronage widely practised at the time. By this custom, wealthy individuals acted as patrons to relatively poorer people lower down the social scale. In fact a person's status and celebrity sometimes rested on the number of clients whom he could support financially. The client was not expected to work for the patron, merely to 'sing his praises' by attendance upon him at certain times and events.

Fawning and flattery were the name of the game.

Now, what if either the client or both the client and his patron were converted to Christ? Then, in Paul's eyes, the usual rules did not apply. A Christian 'client' should not now expect to be supported by a richer patron, even less so if that patron was a fellow-believer.

Living a quiet life (cf 1 Thess. 4:11) meant minding one's own business and ended the practice of clients agitating publicly on behalf of their patrons. The culture of phony dependency and hypocritical relationship was to be broken. Instead, the 'client' should seek to work for his own upkeep and not use his leisure time to meddle in other people's affairs. In this Paul was able to point to his own conduct as a 'model' (vv.7–9) and to his previous teaching to reinforce it (v.6b and also 1 Thess. 5:14).

Paul's supreme aim – as always in his later letters – is to build up the Church as the body of Christ. It is significant that he first addresses the whole church at Thessalonica (vv.6–11) before directly talking to the 'idle' (v.12). In the Church there must be none who are simply and always suppliers and others who are simply and always recipients. *All without exception, according to their own ability, are to be givers.*

3:13-15 Untiring good work

[13]And as for you, brothers, never tire of doing what is right.

[14]If anyone does not obey our instruction in this letter, take special note of him. Do not associate with him, in order that he may feel ashamed. [15]Yet do not regard him as an enemy, but warn him as a brother.

The community's reaction to the 'unruly idle' is strong meat for twenty-first-century churches in which the notion of church discipline has virtually disappeared and any feature of it seems judgmental and unfeeling. The 'unruly idle' should 'have their card marked', be shunned by the fellowship, in order to make the offender 'ashamed'. This is tough love but it is still for brothers and sisters, not enemies. It begs huge questions about the purity and integrity of our church life together.

Gordon Fee wisely comments that if we don't have such a God-filled, grace-soaked fellowship that it would feel like death to leave it, then we had better not apply this injunction. Lacking such a fellowship, the implementation of such words as these may prove only legalistic and authoritarian. But where the family of Christ can speak the truth in binding love, then who knows what reality might burst in on us and who knows what healing and redemption follow?

The world awaits a church like that founded on the original apostolic gospel in Thessalonica, one that truly 'turns that world upside down'. In Bruce Winter's words: 'In his day Paul determined to see the abolition of the patronage system in the Christian community.' But the effect of this was not to make the Christian community into a self-serving ghetto; rather it was to 'create a whole new class of benefactors … who do good without expectation of reciprocity or repayment'.[24] In the last analysis, no one should ever 'tire of doing what is right' in being a benefactor. Love never fails.

3:16–18 Prayer and peace

3:16

[16]Now may the Lord of peace himself give you peace at all times and in every way. The Lord be with all of you.

The Lord of peace give you peace 'at all times and in every way'. Is this really possible? It is, if the Lord of peace Himself is always present with us. 'The peace of Christ does not require a mould of easy circumstances. Galilee in storm and Calvary in darkness both set it off.'[25]

Being a believer is not all about grim determination and dogged persistence. Even the greyest days are transfigured by the presence of a radiant personality. It doesn't take much.

The merest taste of the sweet love that flows from His cross, the slightest surge of the absurd joy of Easter, the most fleeting intake of breath at the exhilarating prospect of His coming, a glimpse of that loving face, an echo of the lordly voice, a hint of that living hope … and we know that He is with us.

To 'be with the Lord for ever' is our glorious destiny (1 Thess. 4:17c). Meanwhile He will never leave us or forsake us as He gets us to the glory.

The much-loved teacher and author, Lewis Smedes, died in December 2002. The last words of his last book were, as always, relentlessly honest and thankfully true:

> This is where I find myself now on the journey that God and I have been on, at the station called hope, the one that comes right after gratitude and somewhere not far from journey's end. It has been 'God and I' the whole way. Not so much because he has always been pleasant company. Not because I could always feel his presence when I got up in the morning or when I was afraid to sleep at night. It was because he did not trust me to travel alone.

Smedes concludes:

> Personally I liked the last miles of the journey better than the first. But, since I could not have the ending without first having the beginning, I thank God for getting me through and bringing me home. And sticking with me all the way.[26]

3:17-18

[17]I, Paul, write this greeting in my own hand, which is the distinguishing mark in all my letters. This is how I write.
[18]The grace of our Lord Jesus Christ be with you all.

Dictation over, Paul takes the quill pen from Silas and adds his own personal greeting in his own distinctive handwriting. Make no mistake, this letter is no forgery. This, he says, is how he writes. This is how he lives. This is how he will be remembered. This is why his words resonate down the centuries so that we can feel the power of peace and enjoy access to grace.

'The grace of our Lord Jesus Christ be with you all' (v.18). In the Christian scheme of things, signing off in this way is no platitude, no mere literary convention. It says all that needs to be said about where we have come from and how we have come, and tells us too about how we are going to make it to where God wants us to be.

Here is the secret of travelling hopefully in the 'meantime'. For grace is not a soft and easy sentiment, a rather bland but comforting sense that God is favourable to us. The great Victorian preacher, J.H. Jowett, made the right connection:

Grace is more than a smile of good nature. It is not the shimmering face of an illumined lake; it is the sunlit majesty of an advancing sea. It is a transcendent and ineffable force, *the outgoing energies of the redeeming personality of God washing against the polluted shores of human need.*[27]

Grace comes to us from God through Jesus Christ not as a nice idea but as mighty force. Picture yourself standing on a beach and watching the foaming breakers rushing in towards you. This is grace. And this grace will keep on coming to us until Jesus comes for us.

Prayer and Reflection

We pray that the message of Jesus as Lord may run riot in the world.
We relish news of the global impact of the gospel.

Lord, in Your faithfulness, protect Your messengers from evil in all its guises; sustain Your persecuted Church in doing good.

Lord, the folk-wisdom of my childhood said that the devil finds work for idle hands.
Lord, we have to admit that left to our own devices we tend to make trouble, not peace.
By the grace that forgives and cleanses us, stimulate us to do good, to be fruitful, to make peace.

I know how worthless being unemployed or made redundant can make you feel.
Teach us not to grade people by the size of their wage-packet or salary but by the value of the work they do.
Thank You for providing me with work and for the satisfaction I gain from doing it well.
Save us all from becoming workaholics, especially those who feel under pressure to perform or on an unrelenting treadmill of demands.
Give us all the courage to observe the Sabbath and find saving space in our lives.

Lord of peace, be our peace at all times and in all circumstances.
Lord, be present with us through the long, slow movements as well as at the crashing crescendo.

Be near me Lord Jesus, I ask you to stay
Close by me for ever, and love me I pray ...

Keep your grace coming, Lord. until Jesus comes,
Amen.

- Draw up a list of instances that illustrate the perseverance of Jesus in face of opposition.
- Find out more about the persecuted Church in today's world, and ask the Lord to tell you what to do about what you discover.

Resources

Karl Paul Donfried, *Paul, Thessalonica, and Early Christianity*, Grand Rapids: Eerdmans, 2002.
Fascinating essays on the cultural setting and theology of the Thessalonian letters.

Gordon Fee, audio-tape series from Regent's College: Vancouver, Canada.
I have drawn heavily on these masterly and inspiring tapes of a much-loved 'scholar on fire'.

Michael Holmes, *1 and 2 Thessalonians*, NIV Application Commentary, Grand Rapids: Zondervan, 1998.
This is a fine example of an increasingly useful series.

John Stott, *The Message of Thessalonians: Preparing for the Coming King*, Leicester: InterVarsity, 1991.
Perhaps the most accessible work for the general reader by an inimitable scholar–preacher.

Ben Witherington III, *The Acts of the Apostles: A Socio-Rhetorical Commentary*, Grand Rapids: Eerdmans, 1998.

Historical background material
Richard Horsley (editor), *Paul and Empire: Religion and Power in Roman Imperial Society*, Harrisburg: Trinity Press International.

This is a series of essays by experts in history and theology, which I find I am turning to again and again in order to visualise Paul and the early churches in their cultural setting.

Craig Keener, *The IVP Bible Background Commentary (New Testament)*, Downers Grove: InterVarsity Press, 1993.
This is a treasure trove for any Bible-lover.

Rainer Riesner, *Paul's Early Period: Chronology, Mission Strategy, Theology*, Grand Rapids: Eerdmans, 1998, pp.337–393.
A unique book packed with information.

Notes

1 Thessalonians

1. A.J. Conyers, *The Eclipse of Heaven: Rediscovering the Hope of a World Beyond* (Downers Grove: InterVarsity Press, 1992), p.111.

2. Peter Taylor Forsyth, *Positive Preaching and the Modern Mind* (New York: Armstrong, 1907), p.47.

3. Historical background on Thessalonica has been gleaned from various sources. In addition to the standard commentaries and Gordon Fee's audio-tape series from Regent's College, Vancouver, Canada, particular use has been made of Rainer Riesner's fascinating research in *Paul's Early Period: Chronology, Mission Strategy, Theology* (Grand Rapids: Eerdmans, 1998), pp.337–393.

4. Michael W. Holmes, *1 and 2 Thessalonians: The NIV Application Commentary* (Grand Rapids: Zondervan, 1998), p.50.

5. Riesner, *Paul's Early Period*, p.357. See also Ben Witherington, *The Acts of the Apostles: A Socio-Rhetorical Commentary* (Grand Rapids: Eerdmans, 1998), p.508.

6. Richard A. Horsley and Neil Asher Silberman, *The Message and the Kingdom: How Jesus and Paul Ignited a Revolution and Transformed the Ancient World* (Minneapolis: Fortress Press, 2002), p.154.

7. Ibid., p.154.

8. Donald B. Kraybill, *The Upside-Down Kingdom* (Scottdale: Herald

Press, revised edn, 1990), p.23.

9. No one sounded this warning more clearly than the late Lesslie Newbigin. See for example his *Foolishness to the Greeks* (London: SPCK, 1986).

10. Os Guinness, 'Mission in the Face of Modernity' in eds. Martyn Eden and David Wells, *The Gospel in the Modern World: A Tribute to John Stott* (Leicester: InterVarsity Press, 1991), p.96.

11. Ibid., p.97.

12. Cited by Craig Carter, *The Politics of the Cross: The Theology and Social Ethics of John Howard Yoder* (Grand Rapids: Brazos Press, 2001), p.205.

13. Kraybill, *Upside-Down Kingdom,* p.272.

14. Stanley Hauerwas and William Willimon, *Where Resident Aliens Live* (Nashville: Abingdon, 1996), p.45.

15. Michael J. Gorman, *Cruciformity: Paul's Narrative Spirituality of the Cross* (Grand Rapids: Eerdmans, 2001), p.357.

16. David de Silva, *The Hope of Glory: Honor Discourse and New Testament Interpretation* (Collegeville: Liturgical Press, 1999), p.93.

17. Mark Buchanan, *The Holy Wild* (Oregon: Multnomah, 2003), p.109.

18. Quoted by Karl Paul Donfried in *Paul, Thessalonica, and Early Christianity* (Grand Rapids: Eerdmans, 2002), p.44.

19. See the commentaries and also Craig Keener, *The IVP Bible Background Commentary, New Testament* (Downers Grove:

InterVarsity Press, 1993), pp.586–587.

20. Fee's judgment is matched by the support given to the reading of the text by John L. White, *The Apostle of God: Paul and the Promise of Abraham* (Peabody: Hendrickson, 1999), p.20. See also Beverley Roberts Gaventa, *First and Second Thessalonians, Interpretation Series* (Louisville: John Knox Press, 1998), p.27.

21. Rodney Clapp, *A Peculiar People: The Church in a Post-Christian Society* (Downers Grove: InterVarsity Press, 1996), p.137.

22. Insightful comments on the images used by Paul in this chapter can be found in Derek Tidball, *Builders and Fools: Leadership the Bible Way* (Leicester: InterVarsity Press, 1999), chapter 5. See also David W. Bennett, *Biblical Images for Leaders and Followers* (Oxford: Regnum Lynx, 1993), pp.80–84.

23. James W. Thompson, *Preaching Like Paul: Homiletical Wisdom for Today* (Louisville: Westminster John Knox Press, 2001), p.51.

24. Ibid., pp.52, 54.

25. Ibid., p.55.

26. See Reisner, *Paul's Early Period*, pp.353–354.

27. Abraham Malherbe, *Paul and the Thessalonians: The Philosophic Tradition of Pastoral Care* (Philadelphia: Fortress Press, 1987), p.50.

28. See my *Leadership: Reflections on Biblical Leadership Today*, second edn (Farnham: CWR, 2002), pp.69–174.

29. In this section I am especially drawing on the fine work of Jeffrey A.D. Weima, "'How you must walk to please God':

Holiness and Discipleship in 1 Thessalonians' in ed. Richard Longenecker, *Patterns of Discipleship in the New Testament* (Grand Rapids: Eerdmans, 1996), pp.98–119.

30. Ibid., p.105.

31. Gordon Fee, Regent's College audio-tape.

32. Thomas Howard, *Hallowed be This House* (Wheaton: Harold Shaw Publishers, 1979), pp.110–111.

33. Ibid., p.108; cf also Gordon Fee, *God's Empowering Presence: The Holy Spirit in the Letters of Paul* (Peabody: Hendrickson, 1994), p.51.

34. In addition to the commentaries see Frank Thielman, *Paul and the Law* (Downers Grove: InterVarsity Press, 1994), pp.73ff.

35. Gordon Fee, Regent's College audio-tape.

36. Nicholas Wolterstorff, *Lament for a Son* (London: SPCK, 1987/1997), p.31.

37. Cited in Howard Clark Kee, *The Origins of Christianity: Sources and Documents* (London: SPCK, 1980), p.264.

38. Austin Farrer, *A Celebration of Faith* (London: Hodder and Stoughton, 1970), p.105.

39. Wolterstorff, *Lament for a Son*, p.86.

40. Ibid., p.63.

41. Richard A. Horsley, 'Paul's Counter-Imperial Gospel: Introduction' in ed. Richard A. Horsley, *Paul and Empire:*

Religion and Power in Roman Imperial Society (Harrisburg: Trinity Press International, 1997), p.146.

42. Forsyth, *Positive Preaching*, p.174.

43. Robert Barron, *And Now I See: A Theology of Transformation* (New York: Crossroad, 1998), p.164.

44. Barry L. Callen, *Authentic Spirituality: Moving Beyond Mere Religion* (Grand Rapids: Baker Books, 2001), p.82.

45. James Denney, *The Epistles to the Thessalonians, The Expositor's Bible* (London: Hodder & Stoughton, 1892), pp.258–259.

46. John Piper, *The Purifying Power of Living by Faith in Future Grace* (Leicester: InterVarsity Press, 1995), p.66.

2 Thessalonians
1. N.T. Wright, *The New Testament and the People of God* (London: SPCK, 1992), p.360.

2. See recently Ann Jervis, 'Accepting Affliction: Paul's Preaching on Suffering' in ed. William P. Brown, *Character and Scripture: Moral Formation, Community and Biblical Interpretation* (Grand Rapids: Eerdmans, 2002), pp.290–316.

3. Both examples are taken from Philip Jenkins, *The Next Christendom: The Coming of Global Christianity* (Oxford: Oxford University Press, 2002), p.218.

4. Gorman, *Cruciformity*, p.346. I have profited greatly from this richly textured study.

5. Os Guinness, *Long Journey Home* (Grand Rapids: Zondervan, 2001), p.57.

6. Two very helpful recent surveys of how to handle apocalyptic language are Brent Sandy, *Plowshares and Pruning Hooks: Rethinking the Language of Biblical Prophecy and Apocalyptic* (Downers Grove: InterVarsity Press, 2002); and Craig C. Hill, *In God's Time: The Bible and the Future* (Grand Rapids: Eerdmans, 2002).

7. Carl Braaten, 'The Recovery of Apocalyptic Imagination' in ed. Carl Braaten and Robert Jenson, *The Last Things: Biblical and Theological Perspectives on Eschatology* (Grand Rapids: Eerdmans, 2002), p.16.

8. Jenson, *Last Things*, pp.38–39.

9. Gordon D. Fee, 'Pneuma and Eschatology in 2 Thessalonians 2:1–2: A Proposal about "Testing the Prophets" and the Purpose of 2 Thessalonians' in ed. Gordon D. Fee, *To What End Exegesis? Essays Textual, Exegetical, and Theological* (Grand Rapids: Eerdmans, 2001), pp.290–308.

10. Ibid., p.300.

11. Michael Burleigh, *The Third Reich: A New History* (London: Macmillan, 2000), p.157.

12. Donfried, *Paul*, pp.58–59.

13. Charles A. Wanamaker, *1 and 2 Thessalonians, New International Greek Commentary* (Grand Rapids/Exeter: Eerdmans/Paternoster, 1990), pp.252–253.

14. Ibid., pp.256–257.

15. Denney, *Epistles to the Thessalonians*, p.341.

16. Horsley and Silberman, *Message*, p.158.

17. Denney, *Epistles to the Thessalonians*, p.348.

18. Jaroslav Pelikan, *The Christian Tradition: A History of the Development of Doctrine, Vol. 1, The Emergence of the Catholic Tradition (100–600)* (Chicago: University of Chicago Press, 1971), p.9.

19. F.W. Faber, 'My God How Wonderful Thou Art', Baptist Hymn Book, no. 64.

20. Wright, *New Testament*, p.359.

21. See Jenkins, *Next Christendom*.

22. John Piper, *Let the Nations Be Glad: The Supremacy of God in Missions* (Grand Rapids: Baker Books, 1993), p.67.

23. Bruce W. Winter, *Seek the Welfare of the City: Christians as Benefactors and Citizens* (Grand Rapids/Carlisle: Eerdmans/Paternoster, 1994), pp.41–60.

24. Ibid., p.60.

25. W.E. Sangster, *The Pure in Heart: A Study in Christian Sanctity* (London: Epworth Press, 1954), p.119.

26. Lewis B. Smedes, *My God and I: A Spiritual Memoir* (Grand Rapids: Eerdmans, 2003), p.178.

27. J.H. Jowett, *Apostolic Optimism and Other Sermons* (London, 1901), p.113, cited by Donald Macleod, *Behold Your God* (Scotland: Christian Focus Publications, 1995), p.142.

National Distributors

UK: (and countries not listed below)
CWR, Waverley Abbey House, Waverley Lane, Farnham, Surrey GU9 8EP.
Tel: (01252) 784700 Outside UK +44 (0)1252 784700

AUSTRALIA: CMC Australasia, PO Box 519, Belmont, Victoria 3216.
Tel: (03) 5241 3288

CANADA: Cook Communications Ministries, PO Box 98, 55 Woodslee Avenue, Paris, Ontario.
Tel: 1800 263 2664

GHANA: Challenge Enterprises of Ghana, PO Box 5723, Accra.
Tel: (021) 222437/223249 Fax: (021) 226227

HONG KONG: Cross Communications Ltd, 1/F, 562A Nathan Road, Kowloon.
Tel: 2780 1188 Fax: 2770 6229

INDIA: Crystal Communications, 10-3-18/4/1, East Marredpally, Secunderabad – 500 026.
Tel/Fax: (040) 7732801

KENYA: Keswick Books and Gifts Ltd, PO Box 10242, Nairobi.
Tel: (02) 331692/226047 Fax: (02) 728557

MALAYSIA: Salvation Book Centre (M) Sdn Bhd, 23 Jalan SS 2/64, 47300 Petaling Jaya, Selangor.
Tel: (03) 78766411/78766797 Fax: (03) 78757066/78756360

NEW ZEALAND: CMC Australasia, PO Box 36015, Lower Hutt.
Tel: 0800 449 408 Fax: 0800 449 049

NIGERIA: FBFM, Helen Baugh House, 96 St Finbarr's College Road, Akoka, Lagos.
Tel: (01) 7747429/4700218/825775/827264

PHILIPPINES: OMF Literature Inc, 776 Boni Avenue, Mandaluyong City.
Tel: (02) 531 2183 Fax: (02) 531 1960

REPUBLIC OF IRELAND: Scripture Union, 40 Talbot Street, Dublin 1.
Tel: (01) 8363764

SINGAPORE: Armour Publishing Pte Ltd, Block 203A Henderson Road, 11–06 Henderson
Industrial Park, Singapore 159546.
Tel: 6 276 9976 Fax: 6 276 7564

SOUTH AFRICA: Struik Christian Books, 80 MacKenzie Street, PO Box 1144, Cape Town 8000.
Tel: (021) 462 4360 Fax: (021) 461 3612

SRI LANKA: Christombu Books, 27 Hospital Street, Colombo 1.
Tel: (01) 433142/328909

TANZANIA: CLC Christian Book Centre, PO Box 1384, Mkwepu Street, Dar es Salaam.
Tel/Fax (022) 2119439

USA: Cook Communications Ministries, PO Box 98, 55 Woodslee Avenue, Paris, Ontario, Canada.
Tel: 1800 263 2664

ZIMBABWE: Word of Life Books, Shop 4, Memorial Building, 35 S Machel Avenue, Harare.
Tel: (04) 781305 Fax: (04) 774739

For email addresses, visit the CWR website: www.cwr.org.uk
CWR is a registered charity – number 294387

Trusted
All Over the World

Daily Devotionals

Books and Videos

Day and Residential Courses

Counselling Training

Biblical Study Courses

Regional Seminars

Ministry to Women

CWR have been providing training and resources for Christians since the 1960s. From our headquarters at Waverley Abbey House we have been serving God's people with a vision to help apply God's Word to everyday life and relationships. The daily devotional *Every Day with Jesus* is read by over three-quarters of a million people in more than 150 countries, and our unique courses in biblical studies and pastoral care are respected all over the world.

For a free brochure about our seminars and courses or a catalogue of CWR resources please contact us at the following address:

**CWR,
Waverley Abbey House,
Waverley Lane,
Farnham,
Surrey GU9 8EP**

**Telephone: +44 (0)1252 784700
Email: mail@cwr.org.uk
Website: www.cwr.org.uk**

CWR CRUSADE FOR WORLD REVIVAL · *Applying God's Word to everyday life and relationshi*